I see that grace groweth best in winter.
—Samuel Rutherford, *Letters*

MARGARET CLARKSON

Grace
Grows
Best
in Winter

Help for those who must suffer

Grason
Minneapolis, MN

Copyright © 1984 Margaret Clarkson
First published 1972 by The Zondervan Corporation
This edition published 1985 by Wm. B. Eerdmans Publishing Company
255 Jefferson S.E., Grand Rapids, Mich. 49503

Library of Congress Cataloging in Publication Data

Clarkson, Edith Margaret, 1915-
 Grace grows best in winter.

 1. Suffering — Religious aspects — Christianity.
I. Title.
BV4909.C56   1985   242′.4   85-1520

ISBN 0-8028-3616-X

The author wishes to thank Moody Press for permission to reprint from her devotional *God's Hedge* (Moody Press, Chicago, 1968), in which parts of chapters 1, 2, 4, 5, 8 through 13, 15, 16, 28, and 31 first appeared.

CONTENTS

FOREWORD

It was not long after I left the hospital in 1967 that I fell into a deep pit of depression. I was but a young girl, yet I was facing an overwhelming future — a life of total and severe paralysis.

I was in desperate need of answers. I knew in a vague sort of way that the answers to my questions were probably squeezed somewhere in the pages between the covers of my Bible. I just needed someone... anyone... who would sit down next to me and help me piece together the puzzle of my heartache and hardship.

A young friend who often came by my home for visits stopped by one day with a special book in hand. As she flipped through its pages for me, she asked if we might read a chapter from this book on a weekly basis. I shrugged my shoulders and commented that would be fine.

Together, we read the book through the weeks of winter. Not only did I welcome my friend's fireside visits, but I eagerly looked forward to each chapter — discovering sense in sovereignty and delighting in a new grasp on God's grace.

Grace. It took root in my life during that first long, lonely winter out of the hospital. And despite... no, because of... my disability, it grows stronger as years go by.

May I be the friend who stops by in your life this day? You have in your hands that same special book that I read back in that first winter of my disability. Grace grew then for me. And through grace, you will grow too!

—JONI EARECKSON TADA

PREFACE

This is a book of help for those who must live with a continuing problem of suffering, of whatever kind. It seeks to lead sufferers so to discover and to embrace the character of God that they will be enabled to live triumphantly within the hedge of suffering wherein He has placed them, and from which in His inscrutable sovereignty He has not yet seen fit to release them.

This is not an "escape" book, nor does it emphasize physical healing, although it frankly accepts the fact that God can and sometimes does heal. It makes no attempt to probe the problem of pain from a philosophical viewpoint, nor is it a book of dialectic. It contains no sentimentality and offers no shallow "comfort."

Suffering is seen as one of God's means of enlarging the soul's capacity for Himself, and sufferers are enjoined to seek God's enabling that they may lose none of the present or future fullness that God would have them experience as a result. This is not the most usual view of human suffering, but I am convinced that it is the only practical, workable way to cope with its stresses.

There is only one way in which a sufferer may come to realize the eternal good which is God's purpose for him in pain, and that is by a close study of the Word of God. Sufferers often find it difficult, even impossible, to maintain any systematic pattern of Bible study; but God in His mercy has

9

not forgotten such needy ones. Scripture abounds with what I like to call God's fragments—a host of all-encompassing minutiae which, though fragmentary and seemingly unimportant in themselves, are nonetheless capable of nourishing and sustaining the seeking soul. I have sought to bring together scores of such tiny references, as well as many larger ones, and to show how they may be used to withstand the stresses of living with pain. For over twenty years I kept a personal notebook in which I jotted down such fragments of heavenly manna as God blessed them to my own soul; and it is from these notes and the strength that such Scriptures imparted that this book has grown.

In order that seekers may be able to realize God's sufficiency from such Bible studies, I have listed, in order, at the end of each paragraph all Scriptures used. Some passages are merely mentioned, others have been paraphrased, and many are quoted directly, but all are listed. If such listings surround this book with an aura that is more studious than literary, I make no apologies: this book makes no pretensions to be anything other than a series of studies by means of which a sufferer may be helped to make contact with God, his only Source of supply, and to find grace to help in time of need. Needy souls will recognize this; and it is for needy souls, not literary critics, that this book has been written. There is some repetition of Scriptures used in these studies from chapter to chapter: as the facets of a diamond shine with differing lights when viewed from different angles, so God's truth illumines our varying human needs. The sufferer will understand such repetition, even if the critics don't: his pain is repetitive and so is his need.

These studies may prove to minister more effectively if they are not read as a unit, but are considered one by one over a period of time. May God enrich the souls of all who seek Him through these humble reflections, and make grace to grow and bring forth its heavenly fruit through the cold and darkness of their winter.

SOVEREIGN LORD!

O Father, You are sovereign
   In all the worlds You made;
Your mighty Word was spoken,
   And light and life obeyed.
Your voice commands the seasons
   And bounds the ocean's shore,
Sets stars within their courses
   And stills the tempests' roar.

O Father, You are sovereign
   In all affairs of man;
No powers of death or darkness
   Can thwart Your perfect plan.
All chance and change transcending,
   Supreme in time and space,
You hold Your trusting children
   Secure in Your embrace.

O Father, You are sovereign,
   The Lord of human pain,
Transmuting earthly sorrows
   To gold of heavenly gain,

All evil overruling,
*   As none but Conqueror could,*
Your love pursues its purpose —
*   Our souls' eternal good.*

O Father, You are sovereign!
*   We see You darkly now,*
But soon before Your triumph
*   Earth's every knee shall bow.*
With this glad hope before us
*   Our faith springs forth anew:*
Our Sovereign Lord and Savior,
*   We trust and worship You!*

MARGARET CLARKSON

1

GOD'S HEDGE

What can we do, o'er whom the unbeholden
Hangs in a night with which we cannot cope?
What but look sunward, and with faces golden,
Speak to each other softly of a Hope?[2]

The four walls of a sickroom can be a confining space, even
when they form the boundaries of one's world for only a short
time. In the hospital or at home, how the soul and body long
to be free, to escape those enclosing walls!

Yet countless people must endure such imprisonment for
weeks, months, years—even a lifetime. Many must be confined
to institutions while others must live in wheelchairs or endure
the loneliness and frustration of blindness, deafness, or other
physical handicaps. Still others, though up and about, possibly
even earning their own living, are compelled to do so with the
utmost difficulty, their whole lives circumscribed by the
stringent necessities laid upon them by a chronic or incurable
illness. And even these are the envy of those who must live
their helpless lives as a burden upon others who must care for
them.

But physical suffering is not the only form of pain. Evils of every kind are attendant upon mortal man; tragedy, death, and destruction surround us on every hand. We may be compelled to watch a loved one suffer year after year or see a fresh and promising young life wither and die. We may have to witness mental deterioration or breakdown, even self-destruction, in friend or family. We may know the nameless sorrow of bearing a retarded or deformed child, or of rearing our children in the nurture and admonition of the Lord only to see them turn from His way to walk the paths of sin or crime. We may have to experience the shadowed loneliness of an unfulfilling marriage or the isolation of sexual inadequacy, deprivation, or deviation. Our lives may be shattered by accident, disaster, or war. We may have to know agony such as that of a young widow, dying of cancer, knowing that she must leave her little ones alone in the world. Of such dark and tragic fabric human life is made, and out of such sufferings our hedges are formed. Nor are God's children excluded from earth's heritage of sorrows.

How non-Christians hemmed in by such circumstances survive, I am at a loss to understand; I can only salute the examples of amazing courage in the face of terrible odds that are sometimes witnessed. For I know that, under similar conditions, many of those who belong to the Savior, whose lives are fully committed to Him, and who seek to live in obedience to Him, are tempted again and again to cry with the weeping prophet of old: "He hath hedged me about, that I cannot get out"; or with the despairing Job: "Why is light given to a man whose way is hid, and whom God hath hedged in?" (*Lam.* 3:7; *Job* 3:23)

Thus, it is to those who find themselves hedged in by physical infirmities or by thorny barriers of other kinds to whom I write in these pages; and I myself speak from within the confines of one of God's hedges.

God's hedges! It is only as we view our restricting circumstances as being placed about us by God's own hand that we can find courage and faith to face the many-faceted strictures of life within our own particular prison. "This thing is from me," were God's words to His ancient people; we, too, must learn to say, "It is the Lord: let him do what seemeth him good." (1 Kings 12:24; 1 Sam. 3:18)

Hedges are thorny; hedges are sharp; hedges are thick and high. Hedges sometimes cause severe allergic reactions in those who so much as touch their innocent-looking leaves. Hedges shut life out and shut pain, fear, and loneliness in. Misunderstanding and frustration thrive within their prickly walls. To live surrounded by an insurmountable hedge is difficult indeed. No wonder Job longed for death!

But—God's hedge! The hedge of His purposing, His planting, His tending—this makes all the difference. "He hath done it," wrote a saint of old, "and I will lay my hand upon my mouth. If any other had done it to me, I could not have borne it."[17] For those who believe in the love and wisdom of a sovereign God, who see His hand in all that concerns them, a God-hedged life, if a somewhat awesome, even a terrible thing, can be wonderful—a life of joy and freedom, a life of peace and praise, a life of thanksgiving and service. An ancient record tells us that those who dwelt among the hedges dwelt there "with the king for his work"; and we, too, may live with the King Himself and share, however inactively, in the work of His eternal Kingdom. (1 Chron. 4:23)

The hedge can cut off the world and confine on every side, but it cannot shut out our view of the skies nor prevent the soul from looking up into the face of God. Indeed, because there is so little else he can see, and because he needs God so badly, the hedged-in Christian, if he will, may possibly learn to see God more clearly and to know Him more truly than his brother who seems to be free to live life more fully.

If we would know the dew of God's presence within our hedges, however, we must be sure that our barriers are not of our own making. Our hedge may be the result of willful sin, or it may be God's way of seeking to prevent us from walking further in our own way, as with wanton Israel when God hedged up her way with thorns and made a wall so that she should not find her paths. Or God may have to break down the hedge we have painstakingly cultivated against His will, or the man-made fortress in which we have trusted for safety, as He did with His disobedient people, whose psalmist complained, "Thou hast broken down all his hedges; thou hast brought his strongholds to ruin." Such hedges can bring no blessing; but the hedge of God's choosing may be a holy, even a fruitful, thing. (Hos. 2:6; Ps. 89:40)

There are two ways of looking at God's hedges. The hedge of physical limitation or other form of suffering we can see all too clearly; but there is another view more easily forgotten but infinitely sweet to the heart that dwells within.

When Satan appeared before the presence of the Lord and was asked if he had considered the godliness and uprightness of Job the Accuser spat forth in outrage and frustration: "Doth Job fear God for nought? Hast not thou made an hedge about him, and about his house, and about all that he hath on every side?" Satan saw what we too often forget: God's hedges are for the protection of His people. (Job 1:6-10)

In Psalm 80, Israel is likened to a vine brought by God out of Egypt and planted and cared for by Him. In contemplating the state of the nation overrun by her enemies, the psalmist cries out: "Why hast thou then broken down her hedges, so that all they which pass by the way do pluck her?" Lacking the protective hedge of God's planting, the vine was robbed of her fruit and the vineyard made desolate. (Ps. 80:12)

God has made a hedge about the life of every believer. The thorns that seem to hem us in are in reality placed there to close us in to God Himself, to protect us from evil, to provide us with sanctuary in the midst of a troubled world.

For most of His children, God's hedges do not seemingly entail suffering, but only protection. For some, however, they mean unending pain and weakness, disappointment and sorrow, varying in degree to total imprisonment. Why this must be so, we may not know; sufficient for us to know that God Himself has hedged us in, and God's hedges are always hedges of protection and blessing. And God Himself, living there both with us and in us, longs to make of our thorny wall a thing of wonder to men and angels and demons, a thing that will one day bring forth holy blossom and fruit to our eternal good and His eternal glory.

Fragrance and fruit from a thorny hedge—how can it be? Only by His Spirit's enabling: "The fruit of the Spirit is love, joy, peace, longsuffering, gentleness, goodness, faith, meekness, temperance"; and that fruit may be borne on any tree if Christ is there. Did not the thorniest tree of all bring forth the holy flower of redemption and the fruit of everlasting life because of Him who gave Himself there for us? How then can we doubt His power to so enrich our thorn that it, too, may know fruition? (Gal. 5:22, 23)

For God does not ask His children to endure anything that He Himself has not first endured. In Jesus Christ the almighty God suffered Himself to be hedged about in a manner we shall never be able to comprehend, let alone be called upon to undergo.

The infinite Creator hedged Himself about with our fallen humanity. Unsullied Purity took upon Himself the abhorrent hedge of mortal sin, which encircled Him ever more closely until it did Him to death for our sakes. Our hedges are placed about us whether we will or not; His was entered into voluntarily for love of us, and from it He brought forth the richest fruit in the universe—eternal life. Cannot He who so willingly endured such unimaginable condescension for love of us be trusted to care for all that concerns us, even the hedges that seem so hard to understand?

If God has entrusted you with a hedge of suffering, let Him teach you how to live within it so that His holy purpose and His life-giving fruit may be fully accomplished through you!

IN ACCEPTANCE LIETH PEACE

He said, "I will forget the dying faces;
The empty places,
They shall be filled again.
O voices moaning deep within me, cease."
But vain the word; vain, vain;
Not in forgetting lieth peace.

He said, "I will crowd action upon action,
The strife of faction
Shall stir me and sustain;
O tears that drown the fire of manhood, cease."
But vain the word; vain, vain;
Not in endeavour lieth peace.

He said, "I will withdraw me and be quiet;
Why meddle in life's riot?
Shut be my door to pain.
Desire, thou dost befool me, thou shalt cease."
But vain the word; vain, vain;
Not in aloofness lieth peace.

He said, "I will submit; I am defeated.
God hath depleted
My life of its rich gain.
O futile murmurings, why will ye not cease?"
But vain the word; vain, vain;
Not in submission lieth peace.

He said, "I will accept the breaking sorrow
Which God tomorrow
Will to His son explain."
Then did the turmoil deep within him cease.
Not vain the word, not vain;
For in Acceptance lieth peace.[3]

2

THE WAY TO PEACE

To those hedged in by illness or crushing sorrow, to find peace is literally essential to survival. Without it, in many cases, life simply could not be tolerated. Under the weight of our burden, perhaps with health already broken, sanity, too, would break, and possibly even suicide follow. Yet many of us struggle for years, seeking peace in a thousand directions, while all the time it waits us close at hand: for truly, "in acceptance lieth peace."

Acceptance! A little word, but what infinite significance it holds for tormented Christian souls! True acceptance can become the wellspring of inner serenity, security, and joy. It can ease our pain, quiet our fears, release our frustrations, fill our sleepless nights with repose, and make even a life of seclusion or helplessness into a life of praise and service.

> God is our true Peace, and He is our sure Keeper when we are ourselves in unpeace, and He continually worketh to bring us into endless peace.[4]

A new Christian, caught up sharply by a seemingly insurmountable obstacle in her life situation, inquired: "Just how much of this do I accept, and from how much do I seek to free myself?" The answer would seem to be something of a dichotomy: "You accept everything, even the worst, completely and permanently; and then you use every possible resource, both human and spiritual, to effect a solution."

This is important in any sufferer's contemplation of acceptance, whether burdened by illness or crushed by other types of sorrow. Peace will never come until we have accepted in totality all that is involved in our suffering, even facing and accepting the fact that the sorrow that has struck us so suddenly may never be removed. We must accept the worst and then hope, and trust, and work for the best.

It must be recognized, however, that acceptance is not submission, with its overtones of submerged rebellion; it is not resignation, with its dangers of ensuing self-pity and the development of a martyr-complex; it is *acceptance* in the fullest sense of the word. Acceptance is taking from God's hand absolutely anything He chooses to give us, looking up into His face in love and trust, even in thanksgiving. Acceptance is knowing that the confines of the hedge are good, even perfect, however painful they may be, simply because He Himself has given then.

> Whate'er my God ordains is right:
>   Holy His will abideth;
> I will be still whate'er He doth,
>   And follow where He guideth.
>   He is my God;
>   Though dark my road,
> He holds me that I shall not fall:
> And so to Him I leave it all.
>
> Whate'er my God ordains is right:
>   He never will deceive me;
> He leads me by the proper path;
>   I know He will not leave me.

> *I take, content,*
> *What He hath sent;*
> *His hand can turn my griefs away,*
> *And patiently I wait His day.*[5]

But how can we learn such acceptance? Certainly it is not to be found within our own human, rebellious hearts. We must seek it earnestly from God, knowing that our Lord is always more ready to give His grace than we are to receive it.

God gives only good; His will and His ways are perfect. If we believe these things implicitly, we must learn to make use of the strength they can impart. We must say them repeatedly to ourselves in our hours of darkness, laying them on our hearts as a healing balm, even though we may not feel their truth being borne out in our experience.

Feeling, in fact, has nothing to do with it; we cling to naked truth and stake our all on that. We repeat these truths, blindly believing with a faith that refuses to be daunted, until one day we discover, often to our own surprise, that there is no longer any shadow of doubt in our hearts—we *know* the truths to which we have been clinging so desperately; at last we have the unshakable assurance that these things are so. God has wrought His work of faith in us and given us the grace of a great acceptance, which cannot be taken from us.

Such an experience may take place within a short time; more likely it will take months—even years. Always it is initiated by an act of will on our part; we set ourselves to believe in the overruling goodness, providence, and sovereignty of God and refuse to turn aside no matter what may come, no matter how we feel. God honors such faith and holy purpose, and sooner or later He "setteth in pain the jewel of His joy"[2] and gives His gift of an acceptance so deep that peace will be ours forever. For no matter how deep the pain or sorrow, His work in us is deeper, and "whatsoever God doeth, it shall be for ever" *(Eccles. 3:14).*

21

Make room for everything which is capable of rejoicing, en-larging or calming your heart . . . but seek nothing. . . . What is taken from you, just let go. God Himself you will keep for ever; or rather, He will keep you.[6]

Have you sought God's grace of acceptance, or are you still fruitlessly pricking yourself against the thorns of your hedge, seeking a way of escape? God's way of escape is to make you able to bear it. Seek His gift, for only with acceptance comes the blessing of His peace. (1 Cor. 10:13)

O FOR A FAITH THAT WILL NOT SHRINK

O for a faith that will not shrink
  Tho pressed by many a foe,
That will not tremble on the brink
  Of any earthly woe;

That will not murmur nor complain
  Beneath the chast'ning rod,
But in the hour of grief or pain
  Can lean upon its God;

A faith that shines more bright and clear
  When tempests rage without,
That, when in danger, knows no fear,
  In darkness feels no doubt;

A faith that keeps the narrow way
  Till life's last spark is fled,
And with a pure and heavenly ray
  Lights up a dying bed;

Lord, give me such a faith as this,
  And then, whate'er may come,
I'll taste e'en now the hallowed bliss
  Of an eternal home.[7]

3

BY HEARING

Acceptance deep enough to bring God's peace into our hearts is never going to be ours until we have learned some of the secrets of faith.

"Now faith is the substance of things hoped for, the evidence of things not seen," we are told at the outset of the New Testament's great roll call of heroes of the faith. "Now faith means putting our full confidence in the things we hope for, it means being certain of things we cannot see," Phillips puts it; while *The New English Bible* renders it thus: "And what is faith? Faith gives substance to our hopes, and makes us certain of realities we do not see." Then the Scripture goes on to tell us that without faith it is impossible to please God. (*Heb.* 11:1, 6)

Only by faith can we be enabled to look beyond the confines of our hedge and see God as a God of love at work in our lives. Faith great enough to transcend the suffering to which we have been committed; faith strong enough to help us bear our crushing burden of frustration or sorrow; faith deep enough to hush our fears—where can such faith be found?

There is only one answer. Paul gives it in Romans 10:17:

25

"Faith cometh by hearing, and hearing by the word of God." If we would find the faith that will enable us to live triumphantly within our sharp-thorned hedges, we must find it in or from the Word of God.

But here the sufferer is faced with a seemingly insoluble problem—a problem peculiar to those who must live with pain and physical weakness or with the stresses of deep sorrow: the very exigencies that make it so imperative that we live deep within the Word of God also make it nearly impossible for us to study it intently, even to read it meaningfully at all. It takes real physical and mental energy to approach the Scriptures in such a way that they may be transmuted into spiritual power, and this strength we do not possess. Inability to concentrate and to assimilate, sievelike memory, even inability to read the printed page for more than a few lines or perhaps not at all—not just today but many days, sometimes every day—how can the needy one beset by difficulties like these absorb enough of the Word of God to produce the fruit of faith he so sorely requires?

Our God is gracious and merciful and will not leave us alone in our need. "I will not leave you comfortless: I will come to you," He has told us. He has promised that they that wait upon Him shall renew their strength, that none of them that trust in Him shall be desolate, and He will make His promise good. God is greater than any problem. (John 14:18; Isa. 40:31; Ps. 34:22)

Many are the ways by which seeking sufferers may "hear" the Word of God. A letter or a visit from a friend may scatter a little of the precious seed. Radio and television can bring Christian ministry into our homes or hospital rooms. Recordings or tapes of great church music, of beloved hymns, of messages by outstanding preachers, of passages of Scripture, even of the whole Bible, are readily available, many of them on loan. Christian books and magazines abound. Few of us today can honestly say that we are unable to hear the Word of God, even though we may be housebound or bedfast.

If we are unable to read and not fortunate enough to have someone to read aloud to us, then memory must serve us. Happy, indeed, is he who has furnished his memory's storehouse richly in days of plentiful harvests! But pain and weakness may have robbed us of sustained passages of Scripture, so that fragments alone are left: what then? It is just here that the Father has proved Himself particularly gracious to a host of sufferers. As after the miracle of the loaves and fishes the Savior commanded His disciples to gather up the fragments that remained so that none of the food should be lost, so God, by His Spirit, uses every fragment of His Word that remains in our consciousness to nourish our longing souls, or feeds us lovingly on other fragments never before discerned. A sentence, a phrase, even a single word of Scripture, applied by the Spirit of God, can sustain us for hours, days, and weeks in time of need. (John 6:12; 14:26)

Such fragments of food may be tiny and may be gleaned from strange and diverse scriptural fields, usually appearing when least expected and often having little meaning for anyone other than the sufferer to whom the Spirit of God has directed them; yet each is the very Bread of Life to the soul who receives it. If the pages of this book seem to overflow with such fragments, or if some fragments seem to be recurrent, it is not by accident, but in hope that sufferers may discover the strength of such nourishment.

There are no graduates in the school of human pain. As long as we must live hedged-in lives, we will be prone to fluctuation in our faith and our ability to endure. All too often we will be faced with the necessity of relearning faith's lessons and of remaking our commitments and renewing our vows. Truths of Scripture that we thought we knew not only by heart but by experience will have to be reapplied to our souls to meet our daily need.

Here fragments of the Word frequently serve a special purpose in the Spirit's ministry. As myriad drops of dew reflect the sun's rays, each with a similar yet totally differing glory, so tiny bits and pieces of Scripture reflect new facets of radiance from long-loved truths to illumine new phases of old sorrows and meet our recurring needs. It is both easy and perilous to neglect or ignore such fragmentary sources of nourishment when we may not have the food to which we are accustomed; we must not despise the day of small things. Fragments of Scripture in the hand of God can minister to our spirits and sustain us through many trials: let us learn to seek them out and use them.

Need I say that "in sunshine weather"[9] we must be diligent in our study of the Word and do everything possible to hide it in our hearts so that the Spirit will have bread to break to us in especially difficult times? Our "hearing" of the Word may always have to be interrupted or fragmentary, but He whose office it is to teach us all things and bring all things to our remembrance can utilize every scrap to meet our need. It is still the will of the Divine Economist that nothing be lost; He will use and multiply every crumb that we have garnered from His Word, but we must be faithful in harvesting what we can.

Sometimes when the concentrated richness of a Scripture passage is so great that, to our dull senses, it seems to hold for us nothing but words, we may find it helpful to stop trying to uncover the lavish layers of its wealth of meaning and simply skim the whole thing lightly, being content to let its stream of gold wash over us without seeking to capture any particular nugget for ourselves. In so doing we may find our hearts refreshed and cleansed by the majestic sweep of its shining truth, even though we may feel that we have carried away very little of it. Sometimes the main thrust of a passage will be brought home to us even through such a cursory reading; but in any case, if we have laid our hearts open to the Holy Word, we can trust the Spirit to bring it to fruition in our lives and to work the miracle of faith in us.

For faith is the fruit of the Spirit. Nothing we can do can create faith in our hearts: it is the work of the indwelling Christ. We can set our wills to believe; we can make use of every possible means of hearing God's Word; but He alone can produce a living faith in our souls. (Gal. 5:22)

Yet that is His delight. The spirit lives in us for just one purpose—to work out in practical experience in our lives the unspeakable riches of the life of Jesus Christ, to the glory of God. If we bring our needy hearts and hedged-in lives before Him in humility and love, He can be trusted to work in us "that which is wellpleasing in his sight, through Jesus Christ," and to fulfill in us "all the good pleasure of his goodness, and the work of faith with power." (Heb. 13:21; 2 Thess. 1:11)

> Faith came singing into my room,
>   And other guests took flight:
> Fear and Anxiety, Grief and Gloom
>   Sped out into the night.
> I wondered that such peace could be,
> But Faith said gently, "Don't you see?
> They really cannot live with me."[8]

THE SHIELD OF FAITH

I bind unto myself today
  The strong Name of the Trinity,
By invocation of the same,
  The Three in One, and One in Three.

I bind this day to me for ever,
  By power of faith, Christ's Incarnation;
His baptism in the Jordan river;
  His death on the Cross for my salvation;
His bursting from the spicèd tomb;
  His riding up the heavenly way;
His coming at the day of doom:
  I bind unto myself today.

I bind unto myself today
  The power of God to hold and lead,
His eye to watch, His might to stay,
  His ear to hearken to my need,
The wisdom of my God to teach,
  His hand to guide, His shield to ward,
The word of God to give me speech,
  His heavenly host to be my guard.

Christ be with me, Christ within me,
  Christ behind me, Christ before me,
Christ beside me, Christ to win me,
  Christ to comfort and restore me;
Christ beneath me, Christ above me,
  Christ in quiet, Christ in danger,
Christ in hearts of all that love me,
  Christ in mouth of friend and stranger.

I bind unto myself the Name,
  The strong Name of the Trinity,
By invocation of the same,
  The Three in One, and One in Three,
Of whom all nature hath creation,
  Eternal Father, Spirit, Word.
Praise to the Lord of my salvation:
  Salvation is of Christ the Lord.[10]

4

SPIRITUAL HEALING

*Especially for those whose limitations are of a
physical nature.*

Having fully accepted what God has sent us does not mean
that we will not make use of every possible means of cure. We
will consult medical services—the best we can find; we will
cooperate completely with our doctors. We will avail ourselves
of psychiatric and counseling services, if required; these, too,
may be God's way of effecting our deliverance. But we will
avoid medical "quacks" and "miracle cures"; and we will not
run from doctor to doctor, pinning our hopes first here, then
there, frantically seeking a means of escape from our hedge at
any cost. Always we will carry within us the assurance of our
deep acceptance. We will not dishonor our Lord by refusing, in
effect, to accept His choice for us should doctors prove unable
to help us.

It goes without saying that the utmost in spiritual resources
should be called upon by any suffering Christian.

First, we must ask God to search and try us and see if any
sin could be causing our illness or impeding our recovery. If

the Spirit reveals anything at all, known or unknown, that sin must be dealt with and ruthlessly put away. Healing often follows such spiritual catharsis, for sometimes a body whose mind is harboring an unforgiving spirit or cherishing an injury has little else wrong with it: these things have manifested themselves in recurring or continuous illness, rather than in overt action; and when the spirit is healed, the body rapidly, or even suddenly, becomes well.

> You must withdraw into yourself a little and keep quiet before the face of God, then look gently and perfectly at God who is so near to us, to let Him see if there is anything in us or near us which must be handed over, and assure Him of our hearty consent to give up everything to Him. Remain exposed to Him in the light of truth simply, in this way, without any investigations or scruples of your own, for as long as God gives grace.[6]

Second, in the Savior's name we must rebuke Satan and claim deliverance from anything in our illness that may be of him. In the strong name of the Overcomer, and through the power of His healing blood, we may accept what God has given us and at the same time cast out the works of the Evil One within us. Satan sometimes seeks to hinder God's work by causing His servants to fall ill; as mature Christians we must not be ignorant of such devices and must be prepared to take a definite stand against him. Only that which is of God in our illness need we accept. While submitting ourselves to God, we must also strongly resist the devil, if we would have him flee from us. (2 Cor. 2:11; James 4:7)

Third, we should seek healing in accordance with true Scriptural teaching. Without a doubt God is just as able to heal today as in Biblical times; indeed, there seems to be a resurgence of such miracles among us in recent years. We should fully acquaint ourselves with what the Bible has to say on this subject and earnestly ask that we, too, may be healed. We must not, however, spend all the scant store of strength we have in praying unceasingly for healing. Before we ask for ourselves, we must pray first for the glory of God and for the advancement of His kingdom and His will. If we do not have enough strength to do both, we must commit our own cause to Him in faith and use our energies in the cause of His kingdom. There are things that are more important than our healing.

When praying for healing, we must remember that from New Testament days right down to the present, God has seen fit to heal some and to withhold healing from others. Paul's thorn in the flesh is a case in point, and the suffering saints of church history bear abundant testimony to the fact that God does not always remove His hedges from the lives of those He loves. We should seek healing, but always undergirding our asking must be our complete acceptance of what God in His sovereign love may see fit to send us. He may say, "Take up your bed and walk," or He may let the thorns of our hedge press more closely about us. To keep running from one healing meeting to the next is to dishonor our Lord, for it shows that we really desire our own will more than His.

When asking for healing, we must "ask in faith," for without faith God cannot heal us; but we must always remember that our faith in itself is no more the means of our healing than it is of our salvation. Faith is necessary for both, but it is God who does the work. He has promised to save all who come to Him in faith for salvation, but I do not find any such all-embracing promise concerning healing. Great anguish is wrought in souls already overborne by pain when well-meaning but misinformed persons assure the sufferer that he must be deficient in faith, otherwise he would be healed. God may see fit to heal one believing soul and leave another, of equal or even greater faith and devotion, to suffer for years; this is His sovereign prerogative. But both the healed and the unhealed should be certain of this: it is God who gives or withholds the gift of healing, and for His own reasons; our

33

faith in itself has nothing to do with it. A clear realization of this can do a great deal to help the sincere believer who has not been healed. *(James 1:6)*

God has many reasons for healing or not healing His suffering ones; some of these reasons are comprehensible to His children, while others are hidden deep within His inscrutability. One of His reasons has to do with His eternal purpose of displaying through His church His mighty wisdom before "the principalities and powers in heavenly places." Just what these spiritual beings are we are not told; but it is clear that God wishes to make a manifestation of His power before them, that He can do so only through His saints, and that He is doing so now, not waiting for the end of the age. *(Eph. 3:10)*

When Christ defeated Satan on Calvary, a new era dawned in the spiritual world. The Prince of Darkness and the last enemy, Death, were vanquished in Christ's death and resurrection. From the moment that He burst forth from the tomb, a new power has been at work in the universe—the power of His endless Life that has triumphed over death and sin. This Life of God manifested in His people is to prove to all beholders that Christ is Strongest of the strong, that His holy power is greater than the powers of evil in the world, that Jesus Christ is Lord.

But this triumph is not yet visible in its totality. Though Christ is now exalted at the right hand of God, sin and death have not yet been divested of their power, but, subject to His will, are allowed to work their evil until the hour of His appearing in final and all-embracing triumph. Until. then, Christ seeks to show forth His victory over death through His people here and now. *(Heb. 2:8)*

Since sickness is a slow form of death, this is one major area of conflict. The powers of death which are still allowed to operate in our lives bring forth illness and, eventually, death. Satan is ever busy at this task, as though by afflicting God's people he might somehow negate his own ultimate defeat. For the present, God permits him a limited power; but He has not left Satan victor on the field. God is at work in the same arena, showing forth through His saints His triumph over death. Thus it pleases Him to deal with death in its slower form of sickness and to heal one Christian here, another there; in this way He reminds Satan that his time is measured and his power restricted.

At the same time, God has chosen to display His power in yet another way. He allows Satan to bring sickness and death into the lives of Christians in order that He may show His strength at an even more critical point—not by healing these sufferers, but by sustaining them in their pain, thus showing Christ's victory by enabling them to triumph over evil even in the midst of it.

This is undoubtedly the reason for much unexplained suffering in the lives of God's people. God is working out His mysterious and eternal purposes through us, using our frail, pain-prone bodies to show His wisdom and His grace before earth and hell and heaven for His own glory. Both by healing and by withholding healing, God is glorified. (Eph. 1:12)

Perhaps you have met all of God's conditions and yet have found no physical healing. This does not necessarily mean that you never will, although in the inscrutable providence of God that may indeed be the case; but it does mean that you must draw closer to the One whose hand has so clearly placed you within the confines of your particular hedge, the One who seeks to be glorified in and through you and who Himself dwells with you in that narrow cell.

Oh, the release, the freedom of those who suffer according to the will of God and have committed the keeping of their souls to Him with the grace of a great acceptance, convinced that God gives only good! Theirs may be the gift of true healing—healing of mind, heart, and spirit—and the peace that the world can neither give nor take away. (1 Pet. 4:19)

Many a sick, weakly soul cowers within a healthy body, while many a hopeless sufferer is perfectly whole in heart. A

35

well body does not preclude inner health, nor does a sick one automatically produce spiritual healing. But the sharp necessities of pain throw one back upon God in a way that holds within it the seeds of a peculiar fruitfulness, while a healthy body may allow even a committed Christian to forget his immense need of God and so become spiritually anemic. A healthy soul is a greater gift than a healthy body, and this is something that none of us need lack.

For the sufferer who, having been denied the gift of physical healing, seeks the grace of spiritual health, all the promises of God stand ready to meet his need. Here there is no withholding of God's gift of healing, and He who cuts out rivers among the rocks and whose eye sees every precious thing has a particular tenderness and care for the spiritual health of those whose bodies He has declined to heal. They who seek his grace in this regard shall not be disappointed, but shall have the true gift of spiritual healing. (Job 28:10)

JOIN ALL THE GLORIOUS NAMES

Join all the glorious names
  Of wisdom, love, and power,
That ever mortals knew,
  That angels ever bore;
All are too mean to speak his worth,
Too mean to set my Saviour forth.

Great Prophet of my God,
  My tongue would bless Thy name;
By Thee the joyful news
  Of our salvation came;
The joyful news of sins forgiven,
Of hell subdued, and peace with Heaven.

Jesus, my great High-Priest,
  Offered His blood and died;
My guilty conscience seeks
  No sacrifice beside:
His powerful blood did once atone,
And now it pleads before the throne.

My dear Almighty Lord,
  My Conqueror and my King,
Thy sceptre and Thy sword,
  Thy reigning grace, I sing:
Thine is the power: behold, I sit
In willing bonds before Thy feet.

Now let my soul arise,
  And tread the Tempter down;
My Captain leads me forth
  To conquest and a crown;
A feeble saint shall win the day,
Though death and hell obstruct the way.[39]

5

THE AMEN WITH THE KEYS

Fear not; I am the first and the last:
I am he that liveth, and was dead; and, behold,
I am alive for evermore, Amen; and have the keys of hell
*   and of death.* (Rev. 1:17-18)

Alexander Whyte, that saintly Scottish preacher of the turn of the century, whose writings enrich the Church of God to this day, wrote a little book in which he gives intimate pictures of some of the persons to whom Samuel Rutherford wrote his heaven-breathed letters during the long years of his exile in "Christ's Palace in Aberdeen."[17] One of his most engaging figures is the Lady Robertland, who seemed to spend her entire life in the presence of "the majestic Figure of the first chapter of the Revelation." She "always spoke of The Amen, who has the keys of hell and of death. 'It seemed all over and gone with me,' she would say, 'but Providence, since The Amen took it in hand, has a thousand and more keys wherewith to give poor creatures like me our rare outgates. . . . He ties terrible knots just to have the pleasure of loosing them off from those He loves.' "[12]

Lady Robertland saw what every suffering saint of God must see—if he is to learn to live triumphantly—that above and beyond the evil that seems to rule in our fallen world, there stands, unshaken and unshakeable, the eternal throne of God; and there, reigning in majesty and power, is "The Amen with the keys," who came back from death, as Rutherford puts it, "with the keys of hell at His proud girdle."[12]

We who suffer today have the Word of God to cast its light upon our mystery of pain, but it was not always so. We would do well to think back on Old Testament times, before the revelation of the throne at the heart of the universe had been given.

The story of Job is the classic example of unexplained suffering. The first two chapters of the Book of Job show us that godly man, called by God Himself "my servant ... a perfect and an upright man, one that feareth God, and escheweth evil," and then take us behind the scenes, disclosing the throne of God and showing Him in His sovereign control of heaven, earth, and hell. Here God consents to entrust Job with terrible, unexplained, and undeserved suffering, that He may manifest to Satan the sufficiency of His own sustaining power. While it may seem as if all the forces of hell are to be loosed upon poor Job, we are shown clearly that the arena is carefully delineated: so far may Satan go, but no farther; and we see that all the resources of the eternal God are to be at Job's command and that complete victory is assured if he will only continue to trust in his God. (Job 1:8)

But none of this is revealed to Job. He must suffer in darkness, his torments shrouded in mystery, utterly unaware of the part he is playing in the drama of human experience in showing forth to tempested souls forever afterwards the triumph of the life of God in the soul of believing man.

The sovereignty of God is the one impregnable rock to which the suffering human heart must cling. The circumstances surrounding our lives are no accident: they may be the work of evil, but that evil is held firmly within the mighty hand of our sovereign God.

"I am the Lord, and there is none else. I form the light, and create darkness: I make peace, and create evil: I the Lord do all these things," He has told us. This does not mean that God is the author of evil, but rather that it is He who controls it. All evil is subject to Him, and evil cannot touch His children unless He permits it. God is the Lord of human history and of the personal history of every member of His redeemed family. He turns the tide of history to His own ends, even using men who do not acknowledge His sovereignty to work His sovereign will. He called Cyrus the Persian His "anointed . . . whose right hand I have holden," for although Cyrus did not worship Him as God, yet God used Cyrus to effect His will. This is the God in whose mighty hand our pain and trials lie. (*Isa. 45:6-7; 45:1*)

He does not explain His actions to us any more than He did to Job, but He has given us what the sufferers of old never had—the written revelation of His sovereignty and love and His manifestation of Himself in the Savior. If those saints could triumph so gloriously without such revelation, shall we who have it go down to defeat?

Let us seek out all that the Scriptures can show us of the majesty of "the Amen with the keys" and give ourselves to the unceasing contemplation of His sovereign power. Let us learn to live the life that is hidden with Christ in God, anchored safe within the veil in the heavenly throne. Let us find there vision to see earth's sufferings in the light of the sovereign Love that holds our every breath in His wounded hands, knowing that whatever He purposes in the trials He sends us, He purposes it in purest love.

> *I desired oftentimes to know what was our Lord's purpose. And fifteen years after and more, I was answered in spiritual understanding, saying thus:* Wouldst thou know thy Lord's purpose in this thing? Know it well: Love was His purpose.

41

Who shewed it thee? Love. What shewed He thee? Love. Wherefore shewed He it thee? For Love. Hold thee therein and thou shalt know more in the same. But thou shalt never know therein any other eternal thing. *Thus was I taught that Love was our Lord's purpose.*[4]

How can God purpose pain for His children out of purest love? This is a mystery our finite minds cannot fathom. But to those who are willing to trust Him and to accept what He sends without question, He will reveal His heart of love; and those who have experienced something of this revelation will know that love is indeed our Lord's purpose. In fact, I wonder if those who suffer most severely are not the ones who are most fully persuaded that all His ways are truly ways of love.

It was from prison, with many sufferings behind him and many yet to come, that Paul wrote to the Ephesian Christians, praying that the Savior would give them some understanding of His immeasurable love and that they "might be filled with all the fulness of God." Again, he wrote to the church at Rome, and to us: "Who shall separate us from the love of Christ? Shall tribulation, or distress, or persecution, or famine, or nakedness, or peril, or sword? . . . Nay, in all these things we are more than conquerors through him that loved us. For I am persuaded, that neither death nor life, nor angels, nor principalities, nor powers, nor things present, nor things to come, nor height, nor depth, nor any other creature, shall be able to separate us from the love of God, which is in Christ Jesus our Lord" *(Eph. 3:17-19; Rom. 8:35 37-39)*

"The Amen with the keys," who plans our "evils" in His heart of unspeakable love, is sovereign in His universe; but it rests with each one of us to say if He is to be sovereign in our lives. As we learn more and more of His sovereign love, may our lives blend with His in an Amen chorus whose music shall echo throughout eternity!

NONE OTHER LAMB

None other Lamb, none other Name,
   None other Hope in heaven, or earth, or sea,
None other Hiding-place from guilt and shame,
   None beside Thee.

My faith burns low; my hope burns low;
   Only my heart's desire cries out in me,
By the deep thunder of its want and woe,
   Cries out to Thee.

Lord, Thou art Life, though I be dead.
   Love's Fire Thou art, however cold I be:
Nor heaven have I, nor place to lay my head,
   Nor home, but Thee.[18]

6

IN ALL POINTS TEMPTED

He said not, Thou shalt not be tempested, Thou shalt not be travailed, Thou shalt not be distressed; but He said, Thou shalt not be overcome.[4]

When Jesus was baptized in Jordan, the heavens were opened, the Spirit of God descended upon Him, and the voice of God Himself was heard, proclaiming to all: "This is my beloved Son, in whom I am well pleased." (Matt. 3:13-17)

But what was the result of this divine in-filling? We might expect to read of wonderful things happening to Jesus following this public acknowledgment of His divine Sonship—but on the contrary, we read a surprising thing: "Then was Jesus led up of the spirit into the wilderness to be tempted of the devil." (Matt. 4:1)

God's fullness had come upon the Savior, not to bring Him honor in the sight of men, but to equip Him for the work of redemption that the Father had given Him to do; and His first assignment following His baptismal anointing was to withstand temptation. He was tempted by Satan, but it was the Spirit of God who led Him into the arena. As with Job, it was

Satan who tempted, but it was God who permitted the temptation.

> God does not tempt or try men in order to know their tempers and dispositions, as if He were ignorant of them; but to exercise their graces, to prove their faith, love and obedience; to confirm and strengthen them by such trials, and to give succeeding ages patterns of obedience, to show them His satisfaction with such as obey, and His displeasure at such as do not.[13]

And so Jesus Himself was tried by temptation. If He was to be a merciful and faithful high priest in things pertaining to God, to make reconciliation for the sins of the people, then in all things it behooved Him to be made like unto His brethren—and this included sharing in that vast area of human experience that involves temptation. Our Savior was in all points tempted like as we are, yet without sin; hence, because He Himself has suffered, being tempted, He is able to succor them that are tempted. (Heb. 2:17; 4:15; 2:18)

To be human is to be tempted, and many and fierce are the temptations experienced by those whom God has hedged in. The presence of the hedge itself constantly tempts us to doubt God, to rebel against the restrictions placed upon us, and to complain. We are tempted in a peculiar way by fear of the future, by apprehension, by depression, by loneliness, by frustration, and by a sense of uselessness. When energy is always too low—even for the minimal tasks of daily living; when constant pain has worn our nerves almost raw; when even the mental and physical resiliency which undergirds the normal person's ability to trust is denied us, how impossible it seems not to succumb to these temptations!

It was when the Lord Jesus was at His lowest physical ebb that He was called upon to withstand the Tempter. For forty days and forty nights He had taken no food. His body was as human as ours, and after such a fast He must have been utterly drained of energy. But then it was that the Father

46

allowed the Evil One to attack Him. By the Word of God and the power of the Holy Spirit, He overcame; and now He lives forever that in Him we, too, may overcome.

God is in control of all the evils that beset us and tempt us to sin, and it is through His permissive will that they are allowed to surround us. The saints of old realized this. "Shall we receive good at the hand of God, and shall we not receive evil?" cried Job, after he had lost his family, his possessions, and, finally, his health. "Shall there be evil in a city, and the Lord hath not done it?" queries the prophet Amos. "This evil is of the Lord," said Elisha calmly when the king's messenger came seeking his life. These men did not look upon the evils as good things, but they knew that they had come in the will of God and that He would keep these strange happenings from harming them. "He doeth according to his will in the army of heaven, and among the inhabitants of the earth: and none can stay his hand, or say unto him, What doest thou?" mused the chastened Nebuchadnezzar. *(Job 2:10; Amos 3:6; 2 Kings 6:33; Dan. 4:35)*

When God placed us within our own particular hedge, He knew well what temptations would cluster around it. But He does not intend that we should be defeated by them, for God is faithful and will not allow us to be tempted beyond our strength, but will with the temptation also make a way to escape, that we may be able to bear it. *(1 Cor. 10:13)*

God makes clear His purposes and His promises concerning temptations. "Count it all joy when ye fall into divers temptations; knowing this, that the trying of your faith worketh patience. But let patience have her perfect work, that ye may be perfect and entire, wanting nothing. . . . Blessed is the man that endureth temptation: for when he is tried, he shall receive the crown of life, which the Lord hath promised to them that love him," wrote the practical James. "Ye greatly rejoice, though now for a season, if need be, ye are in heaviness through manifold temptations: that the trial of your faith, being much more precious than of gold that perisheth . . .

47

might be found unto praise and honor and glory at the appearing of Jesus Christ." Thus the New Testament writers speak victoriously of the endless battle with temptation: its end is glory, for "the Lord knoweth how to deliver the godly out of temptations." (James 1:2-4, 12; 1 Pet. 1:6-7; 2 Pet. 2:9)

Our Savior taught us to pray, "Lead us not into temptation, but deliver us from evil": no man should desire to be tempted. In His inscrutable wisdom, God does allow temptations to come to His children, and He can work eternal good from this trying and refining of our faith; but always He stands ready to deliver us from the evil that Satan would seek to work through such testings. "Yea, though I walk through the valley of the shadow of death," wrote the Psalmist, "I will fear no evil: for thou art with me; thy rod and thy staff they comfort me. Thou preparest a table before me in the presence of mine enemies." He who was in all points tempted like as we are, yet without sin, is able not only to make us stand in the hour of temptation, but is able to spread the feast of victory before those who take their temptations as from Him and trust Him to deliver them. Let us then no longer fear the temptations that surround us, but let us come boldly unto the throne of grace, that we may obtain mercy, and find grace to help in time of need. (Matt. 6:13; Ps. 23:4-5; Heb. 4:15; 4:16)

A SOVEREIGN PROTECTOR I HAVE

A Sovereign Protector I have,
　Unseen, yet for ever at hand,
Unchangeably faithful to save,
　Almighty to rule and command.
He smiles, and my comforts abound;
　His grace as the dew shall descend,
And walls of salvation surround
　The soul He delights to defend.

The work which His goodness began,
　The arm of His strength shall complete:
His promise is Yea and Amen,
　And never was forfeited yet.
Things future, nor things that are now,
　Nor all things below or above,
Can make Him His purpose forego,
　Or sever my soul from His love.

My name from the palms of His hands
　Eternity will not erase;
Impressed on His heart it remains,
　In marks of indelible grace.
Yes, I to the end shall endure,
　As sure as the earnest is given;
More happy, but not more secure,
　The glorified spirits in heaven.

Inspirer and Hearer of prayer,
　Thou Shepherd and Guardian of Thine,
My all to Thy covenant care
　I sleeping and waking resign.
If Thou art my Shield and my Sun,
　The night is no darkness to me;
And fast as the moments roll on,
　They bring me but nearer to Thee.[26]

7

RAISE A MEMORIAL!

When the first round of cataclysmic disasters befell Job, we read that "Job arose, and rent his mantle, and shaved his head, and fell down upon the ground, and worshipped, and said, Naked came I out of my mother's womb, and naked shall I return thither: the Lord gave, and the Lord hath taken away; blessed be the name of the Lord." At his second calamity, when urged by his wife to curse God and die, Job replied, "What? shall we receive good at the hand of God, and shall we not receive evil?" In these two sublime utterances, Job put on record his faith in God and his determination to trust Him whatever might come. There were many times later when Job questioned God and complained bitterly against Him, but never did he reach the point of cursing Him. Was it because the memory of those earlier statements restrained him? He had raised a memorial to his God and to his faith in Him: did it strengthen him against future trials? Was this perhaps the reason that it was to Job that God gave the revelation, until then almost completely shrouded, of man's immortality?— "For I know that my redeemer liveth, and that he shall stand at the latter day upon the earth: And though after my skin worms destroy this body, yet in my flesh shall I see God: Whom I shall see for myself, and mine eyes shall behold, and not another; though my reins be consumed within me." *(Job 1:20-21; 2:10; 19:25-27)*

Often we read of God's people raising a memorial to commemorate some special transaction with God.

When God appeared to Jacob as he fled from Esau's anger, promising His covenant blessing, Jacob made of his stony pillow an altar, made a vow to God, and named the memorial Bethel, the House of God, a name that God was later pleased to honor, calling Himself the God of Bethel. Later, when Jacob, returning to Canaan, was overtaken by the angrily pursuing Laban and a covenant of friendship was made between the two men, they raised an altar to be "the heap of witness" to their vows, offered a sacrifice, and called the place Mizpah. Jacob marked the place where God's angels met him by naming it Mahanaim, saying "This is God's host"; and he marked the place where he wrestled with God by naming it Peniel: "the face of God." When Joshua led Israel across Jordan, one man from each tribe took a stone from the river bed as a sign to the nation and a memorial for future generations that God had opened a path for His people through the midst of the flooding river. Samuel raised the stone Ebenezer, "Hitherto hath the Lord helped us," to commemorate a victory over the Philistines. Again and again God's people went on public record as to their past dealings with God and their faith and covenant with Him for the future. (Gen. 28:17-22; 31:13; 31:48-54; 32:1-2; 32:30; Josh. 4; 1 Sam. 7:12)

It was God Himself who instituted the sealing of a covenant with some tangible memorial. When He established His covenant with Noah following the flood, He gave the rainbow as a token. He instituted the Passover feast as a memorial of Israel's deliverance from death and bondage. When He gave the law to Moses, He wrote it with His own hand upon two "tables of testimony," which Israel could see and remember;

and when Moses broke these in his anger at Israel's sin, God wrote His law a second time on tablets of stone that were later enshrined in the Ark of the Covenant and kept in the innermost room of the Tabernacle. The Ark itself, and the cloud that hovered above it, was a symbol of God's holy presence—something visible to remind Israel of her unseen God. (Gen. 9:12-13; Exod. 12 :1-28; 32:15; 34:1)

It was the Lord Jesus who declared that Mary's gift of spikenard should be told as a memorial for her wherever the Gospel should be preached throughout the whole world; and He also gave to His church the holiest memorial of all, the Lord's Supper, in which, in remembrance of our Savior, we "shew the Lord's death till he come." (Matt. 26:13; 1 Cor. 11:26)

And what about you? God has seen fit to enclose your life within some sort of painful hedge, and you have accepted His will. You have sought release from your prison in healing, but it has not been granted; and you have accepted that. You have bowed before God's sovereignty and worshiped—but have you raised a memorial to your covenant with God? Have you sought the strength that can be yours by writing down your pledge of love and trust and signing it, perhaps in the presence of another Christian? Such a memorial need not necessarily be a public thing: a letter to a close friend or perhaps to your pastor; an entry in your diary; a spoken witness made within the close fellowship of a small praying circle of friends—just a deep, quiet witness to your acceptance of God's sovereignty in your life—this can become your "heap of witness."

Such a memorial can be an anchor to the soul when waves of trouble wash high. When pain is so severe or sorrow so crushing that you cannot articulate your prayer to God, you can at least remind Him of that memorial-covenant, articulated in time of greater strength and clarity of mind, and murmur, even if almost wordlessly: "O God, keep me faithful to that!"—and then rest your heart upon the faithfulness of the One whose covenant with you was signed in His own blood.

IN PAIN

Lord Jesus, King of pain,
  Thy subject I;
Thy right it is to reign:
  Oh, hear my cry,
And bid in me all longings cease
Save for Thy holy will's increase.

Thy right it is to reign
  O'er all Thine own;
Then, if Thy love send pain,
  Find there Thy throne,
And help me bear it unto Thee,
Who didst bear death and hell for me.

Lord Jesus, King of pain,
  My heart's Adored,
Teach me eternal gain
  Is Love's reward:
In Thee I hide me; hold me still
Till pain work all Thy perfect will.[1]

8

WHEN PAIN MOVES IN TO STAY

Ye are Christ's debtor for all providences of this kind, even in
that He buildeth an hedge of thorns in your way: for so ye see
that His gracious intention is to save you (if I may say so)
whether ye will or not.[17]

So the time has arrived when you know that pain has come
to you, not as a temporary lodger, but as a permanent guest,
perhaps even as master of your house of life.

The realization may have been years in the making or it
may have come in one swift, devastating stroke. But at last you
know that pain—your pain, whatever it may be—is to be
yours forever. God's hedge has closed about you on all sides
with what seems to be a terrible and terrifying finality.

Pain for you may be physical, or it may be one of countless
forms of suffering. Your illness may have been diagnosed as
inoperable cancer. Death may have robbed you of one you
loved more dearly than life, or its dread shadow may be
hanging over such a one. Your baby may have been born a
mongoloid or with a hopelessly deformed body. The one to
whom you have joined yourself in the bonds of what you had

thought would be a truly Christian marriage has proved unworthy of the trust. Your child may have rebelled against God and deliberately turned aside to walk the ways of sin. The savings of a lifetime may have been swept away or your means of livelihood suddenly cut off. You may be compelled to watch a dear one undergo long years of physical or mental torment and be helpless to assuage his grief. You may have fallen into a deep depression, undergone a nervous breakdown, even total mental collapse, and doctors have been unable to do much to assist you in your struggle to regain emotional stability. The horror of suicide may have invaded your home or your circle of friends, or you yourself may walk daily in its spectral shadow. Human suffering wears a thousand guises, and in gathering them together under the single term "pain," I include all types of mortal ills. Whatever your sorrow, whatever constitutes God's hedge of thorn for you, His grace alone is sufficient to make you stand. Let us then examine His means of deliverance, no matter what particular form of pain yours may be.

Fear is perhaps the first companion that will make its chill presence felt as God's hedge closes about your life. And fear does not seem to lose its power to alarm even after many years of living with God inside the hedge of His choosing.

> *Let no man think that sudden in a minute*
> *All is accomplished and the work is done:*
> *Though with thine earliest dawn thou shouldst begin it,*
> *Scarce were it ended in thy setting sun.*[2]

Only a daily, hourly, even momentary placing of our extremity in His strong hands can protect us from the crippling ravages of fear. The countless "fear nots" of Scripture, which cover the whole spectrum of human experience, must be taken to ourselves one by one as needed, must be laid upon our hearts and repeated in the presence of this enemy of our souls, even though we may have absolutely no feeling of their strengthening power at the time. What we feel, after all, has nothing to do with the matter; it is the faithfulness of God with which we have to do, and we must learn simply to count His promises as true and carry on accordingly, whether He grants us deliverance from our fears or not. We "reckon" on His Word, as we would reckon up an account in mathematics, and count the answer as true quite apart from any feeling, just as we accept a mathematical calculation that has been done according to rule. In time, assurance will come; but we must learn to live victoriously in the presence of fear and be prepared to do sharp battle with it intermittently, for it is likely to be with us as long as we are hedged about with pain.

> Think and care in no wise about what is to come. Love and suffer in the present moment, thinking more about God and His strength than of yourself and your weakness. If increase of suffering comes, increase of grace will come also.

> Do not think ahead and do not look back! Both bring unrest and are harmful. . . . The present moment must be your dwelling-place. There only can we find God and His will.[6]

We must learn not to be afraid of fear itself, even though we may be all too well aware of its crippling power. "Neither fear ye their fear, nor be afraid," was God's word to His people long ago. "Sanctify the Lord of hosts himself; and *let him be your fear*, and let him be your dread. And he shall be for a sanctuary." The Christian need know only one fear, and that is "the fear of the Lord" or fear of sin. When God is our only fear, we will find that He will be a sanctuary to us to shelter and protect us, to hallow the very pain that drives us to Him for refuge. (Isa. 8:12-14)

"My heart is fixed, O God, my heart is fixed," cried the psalmist. To the soul that deliberately fixes itself in blind, desperate determination upon God shall at length be made known the truth of David's second exultant declaration: "He shall not be afraid of evil tidings: his heart is fixed, trusting in

the Lord. His heart is established, he shall not be afraid."
Gradually this will become true in the lives of those who set
themselves to fight fear with the faithfulness of God. "The life
which I now live," someone has happily paraphrased Galatians
2:20, "I live *by the faithfulness* of the Son of God, who loved
me and gave Himself for me." It is His faithfulness alone that
can enable us to sup daily at the table spread before us in the
presence of our enemies. (Ps. 57:7; 112:7-8; 23:5)

Discouragement and doubt walk hand in hand with fear, and
despondency is its twin sister. Frustration, often overwhelming in its intensity, is its bosom friend; and with it walks an
evil that will undermine our very existence, if we let it—a
sense of worthlessness because we are unable to fill a normal
role in life. Misunderstanding meets us on every side; the
effects of the ceaseless pressures of pain on the human personality cannot be understood by another, and we suffer the
agonies of misunderstanding over and over again. The heartbreak of the constant rising and ebbing of the tides of human
hope within us keeps these evils ever near us. They must be
fought with the same weapons as fear—fought continuously
and unremittingly. Their presence can serve to make us lean
more closely upon our God; in this capacity, they may be
messengers of His peace. "In weakness power is made perfect"
so Williams translates 2 Corinthians 12:9.

Loneliness is one of the hardest of pain's companions to
learn to live with, but it is always present in sorrow or sickness. "I sat alone, because thy hand was upon me," mourned
the weeping prophet. No matter how well-placed we may be
with regard to family or friends, when we suffer, we suffer
alone. Not our nearest or our dearest can feel the pain that
racks our bodies or our minds, compassionate and loving
though they may be. No one else can know our loss or our
heartache, sympathize as they will. Suffering is essentially within oneself; it cannot be communicated to or experienced by
another. To suffer is to be alone—utterly, completely alone.
(Jer. 15:17)

But there is One who can enter into our pain—the solitary Man who was despised and rejected by men—a man of sorrows who was acquainted with grief. He sounded a depth of loneliness and agony such as no mortal has ever known; for was He not forsaken by the Father in that dark hour when, alone upon the cross, He bore the sins and sorrows of the whole, aching world? *(Isa. 53:3)*

> *Yea, once Immanuel's orphaned cry His universe hath*
>   *shaken—*
> *It went up single, echoless: "My God, I am forsaken."*
> *It went up from the Holy's lips, amid His lost creation,*
> *That, of the lost, no son should use those words of*
>   *desolation!"*[15]

Only Christ's cry of anguish is echoless; we who suffer today find His answer to our cry and know that we are not alone. The orphaned cry of Immanuel, God with us, swallows up every cry of the human heart and brings us His sustaining presence. He understands our pain and all its implications as no one else ever can, and He fellowships with us in its dread bonds. I sometimes wonder if we could ever experience such close and precious companionship in any other way!

A sufferer once "raised a memorial" concerning a lifetime of suffering by writing the following thoughts on the matter:

"I am God's by right of creation, preservation, and redemption. Therefore He may do with me as He wills. To many of His creatures He sends health and strength; to me He has sent illness and pain from childhood. This I must accept as His gift, the gift of an all-loving, all-powerful, and all-wise Sovereign-Creator. 'Shall the thing formed say to him that formed it, Why hast thou made me thus?' 'As for God, His way is perfect.'

"Second, I believe that I must accept pain not only as being *in* the will of God for my life, but as *the will of God* for my life. This is the background against which I must show forth

59

His praise. Why this is so, I may not seek to know; I must accept it without question. More, I must know that His will for me is not only good and acceptable, but perfect. I must seek not only to accept it, but to embrace it, knowing that therein lies my highest good.

"To this end I may not pray overmuch for the removal of pain, nor even for its cessation, but rather for the strength to bear it, grace to benefit from it, and devotion to offer it up to God as a sacrifice of praise. I do not doubt for a moment that God is able to heal me absolutely in the flash of an instant; but He has not seen fit to reveal this as His will for me, and I must be content to leave the matter entirely in His hands. The scant strength I have for prayer must not be dissipated in seeking physical blessings, but rather be spent in seeking spiritual growth.

"Third, I believe that pain may be a way of knowing God. Through pain I may have fellowship with Jesus Christ, who, 'though He were a Son, yet learned . . . obedience by the things which He suffered.' Certain it is that the King of Glory is also the King of Pain, and that they who will reign with Him must also suffer with Him. For most people this suffering is not of a physical nature; but is it not possible that for others it may be just that? 'That I may know Him, and the power of His resurrection and the fellowship of His sufferings' must ever be the goal of every true follower of Christ. It may be presumptuous to suppose that one who is appointed to much physical pain can hope to know Jesus Christ in a special bond of the fellowship of suffering; but if the pain is seized upon as an opportunity to know God in this way, I believe He will meet the seeker there. It is possible that such a one may come to know Him in a way that the completely well person perhaps can seldom, even never, experience or understand.

"Fourth, I believe that pain may lead to a deeper prayer fellowship with God than may otherwise be easily experienced. When in the grip of severe pain, there is but one word my heart can utter, and that is the beloved Name, Jesus. For hours at a time I will wordlessly cry to Him, seeking only to stay my soul upon Him, too exhausted to make any request of Him; and at such times I know more complete communion with Him than at any other time in my prayer life. As George Macdonald puts it: 'O God! I cried, and that was all. But what are the prayers of the whole universe but expansions of that one cry? It is not what God can give us, but God that we want. . . . He who seeks the Father more than anything He can give is likely to have what he asks, for he is not likely to ask amiss.'

"Fifth, I believe that pain may provide a way of serving God. One of the hardest things to take about experiencing much physical pain is that it usually precludes much, if not all, active Christian service. I wonder if the pain itself may not be a source of service to God. True service is spiritual, consisting not so much in doing as in being; and the quality of service one may bring is not determined by its quantity, nor by much activity. If a soul that has been taught to suffer can look up into the face of the Savior and not only accept severe pain as from His hand, but thank Him for it, knowing that it is good, even perfect, just because it comes from Him, may not that soul be offering to God one of the purest forms of worship and service known to the spirit of man?

"Finally, I believe that pain may be a training ground for future active and eternal service. 'If in this life only we have hope in Christ, we are of all men most miserable'—this is especially true of the sufferer. The knowledge that pain forbids us much active Christian service in this sphere is one of its sharpest pangs. But this sphere is not all. Time is short, and Eternity is forever; and in that 'last of life for which the first was made,' 'His servants shall serve Him.' May not the sufferer who has known the sharp graving tool of pain in this life find that he has been fitted for some special type of active future service for which no other preparation would have been adequate?

" 'To what purpose is this waste?' is the cry that is wrung

from every human heart that must walk the way of pain. Physical suffering, with its accompanying disappointment, loneliness, loss, misunderstanding, and haunting fears, with its blighted hopes, its thwarting of earnest purpose, its wearing away of life in seeming uselessness—'to what purpose is this waste?'

"In the perfect economy of God, there is no waste—unless I choose to deny Him the right to turn my pain into everlasting good.

"I believe that in eternity, God's glorious fulfillment, His end, will more than justify His strange and difficult means; even the pain-filled life, if given back to Him in love and trust, will be made to show forth the praise of the glory of His grace.

"God keep me momentarily constant in this commitment and faithful to the totality of surrender that it demands!"[16]

How unable we are in ourselves to realize these mighty truths! But we do not seek such victory alone. Another, who dwells both with us and in us has covenanted to keep our hedged-in house in order. As we bring our utter insufficiency to Him, we find Him more than adequate to meet our every need. (John 14:17)

NOTHING IN THE HOUSE

Thy servant, Lord, hath nothing in the house,
Not even one small pot of common oil;
For he who never cometh but to spoil
Hath raided my poor house again, again,
That ruthless strong man armed, whom men call Pain.

I thought that I had courage in the house,
And patience to be quiet and endure,
And sometimes happy songs; now I am sure
Thy servant truly hath not anything,
And see, my song-bird hath a broken wing.

.   .   .   .   .

My servant, I have come into the house—
I who know Pain's extremity so well
That there can never be the need to tell
His power to make the flesh and spirit quail:
Have I not felt the scourge, the thorn, the nail?

And I, his Conqueror, am in the house,
Let not your heart be troubled; do not fear:
Why shouldst thou, child of Mine, if I am here?
My touch will heal thy song-bird's broken wing,
And he shall have a braver song to sing.[3]

9

SAILS TO A SHIP

His cross is the sweetest burden that ever I bare; it is such a burden as wings are to a bird, or sails are to a ship, to carry me forward to my harbour.[17]

"All things work together for good," people are quick to tell others in trouble; some even seek to quiet their own fears with these familiar words.

But even many true Christians frequently omit the significant and qualifying words that follow: "to them that love God, to them who are the called according to his purpose." And few are willing to trace the promise from its source to its final culmination, and to accept the fact that the called of God are predestinated to a high and holy destiny, that of being conformed to the image of His Son. "For whom he did foreknow, he also did predestinate to be conformed to the image of his Son, that he might be the firstborn among many brethren. Moreover whom he did predestinate, them he also called; and whom he called, them he also justified: and whom he justified, them he also glorified." God's purpose for His children is clear: it progresses from the far reaches of eternity through foreknowledge, predestination, calling, and justification to glory; and it is to this good, and this alone, that God has promised to work out the details of our lives. (Rom. 8:28-30)

Mortal man cannot hope to reach such a destiny without learning much of the cross by which his Savior became the firstborn among many brethren that He might bring many sons unto glory. It is to those who are willing to let His cross do its work deep in their lives that the earlier promise, as well as the glorious assurance that follows, is given. Such a realization of the purpose of the cross in their lives is essential to those who must live within God's hedges. (Rom. 8:29; Heb. 2:10)

> Our miseries, however deep and unspeakably numerous, shall in no wise hinder us, but rather urge us on to sink away from ourselves and surrender ourselves to the love of God. . . . His wise and powerful hands can build up on our nothingness a great house of holiness to His everlasting glory.[6]

This is a great truth; but it is also true that pain does not automatically work such blessed alchemy in the lives of believers. We must actively cooperate with God, must learn to embrace His cross and allow Him, even importune Him, to work His total will in us. We must realize that God's purpose in redeeming us is not primarily to make us happy, or healthy, or free from trouble, but to make us holy, to make us like His Son. We must not only accept what suffering He may see fit to send into our lives, but actually seize upon it as a means of bringing about within us that conformity to His image in which, finally perfected, we shall serve and glorify Him throughout eternity.

This does not mean that we need to go looking for trials as a means of sanctification; God will care for our needs in this regard! But it does mean that as we accept our hedges from Him, we do so in the full knowledge of what He desires to accomplish in us through them, and we lay hold upon God to

perfect that which concerns us, that none of our painful learning experiences may be lost. What a tragedy should we suffer
and not realize God's full purpose in our pain! "I will not let
thee go, except thou bless me" must be our attitude toward our
suffering and our God. *(Ps. 138:8; Gen. 32:26)*

Samuel Rutherford, one of the greatest of the men of the
Scottish Covenant, who suffered much for Christ's sake, writes
tellingly and with great discernment of the work of the cross in
the human heart, and this danger of loss does not escape him:

> Give not away your crosses for nothing. . . . Some are to
> answer to the Majesty of God for the abuse of many good
> crosses, and rich afflictions lost without the quiet fruit of
> righteousness. . . . with crosses He figureth and portrayeth us
> to His own image, cutting away pieces of our ill and cor-
> ruption. Lord, cut; Lord, carve; Lord, wound; Lord, do any-
> thing that may perfect Thy Father's image in us and make
> us meet for glory![17]

The soul who seeks to use the suffering God sends as a
means of knowing Him and allowing Him to work out His
purposes in his life will be taught deep lessons by his Master.

> Oh, what I owe to the file, to the hammer, to the furnace of
> my Lord Jesus. . . . Why should I start at the plow of my
> Lord, that maketh deep furrows on my soul? I know that He
> is no idle Husbandman: He purposeth a crop![17]

The cross is given to us "for the perfecting of the saints . . .
till we all come in the unity of the faith, and of the knowledge
of the Son of God, unto a perfect man, unto the measure of
the stature of the fulness of Christ." Its work in us is that of
"perfecting holiness in the fear of God." By it we are privi-
leged to share in the life of Christ Himself, to "suffer with
him, that we may also be glorified together." Shall we not
welcome, even if with a human shrinking of spirit, any means

that God may use to effect such eternal good in us? (*Eph. 4:12-13; 2 Cor. 7:1; Rom. 8:17*)

Eventually the earnest scholar in the school of pain may come so to love and to trust his heavenly Tutor that he will be enabled to look upon his cross as a holy and precious thing because of the fellowship it has brought him with his Lord.

> *Seeing Christ hath fastened heaven to the far-end of the cross, and He will not loose the knot Himself, and none else can (for when Christ casteth a knot, all the world cannot loose it), then let us count it exceeding joy when we fall into divers temptations. . . . Welcome, cross of Christ!*[17]

Do these words from the heart of a sufferer fall strangely upon your ears, perhaps even mock you in your pain? Ask God to help you to lay hold upon Him to work out the full meaning and purpose of His cross in your life, remembering that "the weightiest end of the cross that is laid upon you lieth upon your strong Savior."[17]

> *When I first came to Christ's camp I had nothing to maintain this war, or to bear me out in this encounter. . . . But since I find furniture, armour and strength from the consecrated Captain, the Prince of our salvation, who was perfected through suffering, I esteem suffering for Christ a king's life. I find that our wants qualify us for Christ. . . . Acquit yourself manfully for Christ; spill not this good play. Subscribe a blank submission and put it into Christ's hands. . . . Win Christ's bond (who is a King of His word), for a hundredfold more even in this life.*[17]

Is such triumph possible? Countless thousands whose lives have been lived inside thorny hedges have proved that it is. Numberless others have gone down to defeat in their suffering. Will you be among the victors? Let God teach you to "take the crabbed tree of the cross handsomely on your back," and you will find it "such a burden as wings are to a bird or sails to a ship."[17]

We who suffer have the cross in any case, and nothing we can do can free us from it. How sad to suffer noncreatively, nonredemptively! Let us not stop short of seizing the blessing the cross was designed to bestow: to carry us forward to our heavenly harbor!

MEASURE THY LIFE

If, impatient, thou let slip thy cross,
Thou wilt not find it in this world again,
Nor in another. Here, and here alone,
Is given thee to *suffer* for God's sake.

In other worlds we shall more perfectly
Serve Him and love Him, praise Him, work for Him,
Grow near and nearer Him with all delight;
But then we shall not any more be called
To suffer, which is our appointment here.

Canst thou not suffer then one hour—or two?

If He should call thee from thy cross today,
Saying, "It is finished, that hard cross of thine
From which thou prayest for deliverance,"
Thinkest thou not some passion of regret
Would overcome thee? Thou wouldst say, "So soon?
Let me go back and suffer yet awhile
More patiently—I have not yet praised God."
And He might answer thee, "No, never more.
All pain is done with."

    Whensoe'er it comes,
That summons that we look for, it will seem
Soon, yea, too soon. Let us take heed in time
That God may now be glorified in us;
And while we suffer, let us set our souls
To suffer perfectly: since this alone,
The suffering, which is this world's special grace,
May here be perfected and left behind.

Measure thy life by loss instead of gain;
Not by the wine drunk, but the wine poured forth;
For love's strength standeth in love's sacrifice;
And whoso suffers most hath most to give.[24]

10

PERFECT THROUGH SUFFERINGS

In the first chapter of his letter to the Hebrews, the inspired writer paints a majestic picture of the preincarnate Christ, "God of God, Light of Light, very God of very God,"[19] in all the glories of His coequal existence with the Father; depicts Him in His creative and redemptive activities; and then ascribes to Him the seat of power on the everlasting throne.

But in chapter two we are given a different picture.

"But now we see not yet all things put under him. But we see Jesus, who was made a little lower than the angels for the suffering of death, crowned with glory and honour; that he by the grace of God should taste death for every man. For it became him, for whom are all things, and by whom are all things, in bringing many sons unto glory, to make the captain of their salvation perfect through sufferings." Later we read of His holy priesthood, but the text goes on to describe Him in His ordination to that office: "In the days of his flesh, when he had offered up prayers and supplications with strong crying and tears unto him that was able to save him from death, and was heard in that he feared; though he were a Son, yet learned he obedience by the things which he suffered; and being made

71

perfect, he became the author of eternal salvation unto all them that obey him." *(Heb. 2:8-10; 5:7-9)*

It is not surprising that we should suffer. We live in a fallen world where suffering has entered because of sin, and all mankind, indeed all creation, suffers. Christians are not exempt from suffering; rather, they are distinctly promised that suffering is to be their lot. "Think it not strange concerning the fiery trial which is to try you," writes Peter, and Paul declares that we are "appointed" to afflictions and tribulations. The Church of God has always been a suffering people, and if we read history correctly it would seem that God's choicest saints have frequently been called upon to bear the greatest suffering. God does not explain this; nowhere does the Bible attempt to "justify the ways of God to men."[20] Instead, it shows us the sinless Savior ascending by the pathway of suffering to the eternal throne. *(1 Pet. 4:12; 1 Thess. 3:3)*

Was the Son of God lacking in perfection that He had to learn obedience and be made perfect through suffering?

> Our Lord undoubtedly possessed the disposition of obedience from the beginning of His days on earth. It was, however, in the school of suffering that He learned the practice of obedience. . . . Exemption from suffering would have meant exemption from leadership.[21]

If the Holy One had to be perfected through sufferings before He could become the Captain of our Salvation, shall we poor sinful creatures of dust murmur if our hedges are sharp with thorns or if our pathway to heaven be red with blood?

The Lord Jesus knew what it was to pray with strong crying and tears, even in agony and blood, for a deliverance that could not be granted if He were to become the Savior of the world. He knew the reality of fear as He faced the cross, with all its physical terrors, and the horror of separation from the Father as He became sin for us. He knew loneliness as He walked among men and the ultimate loneliness as He hung forsaken on the cross. He experienced misunderstanding even from those who were His closest friends. He suffered death and hell itself, counting it all joy that we, too, might one day be with Him at the right hand of the throne of God. Then He ascended triumphantly on high, leading captivity captive and receiving gifts for men. *(Heb. 5:7; 12:2; John 17:24; Ps. 68:18; Eph. 4:8)*

"Seeing then that we have a great high priest, that is passed into the heavens, Jesus the Son of God, let us hold fast our profession. For we have not an high priest which cannot be touched with the feeling of our infirmities, but was in all points tempted like as we are, yet without sin. Let us therefore come boldly unto the throne of grace, that we may obtain mercy, and find grace to help in time of need." "For in that he himself hath suffered being tempted, he is able to succour them that are tempted." *(Heb. 4:14-16; 2:18)*

The sufferings and mighty ministry of our great High Priest make the trials of our little hedges appear so small! Yet not a whisper, not a moan, from the least of His suffering ones escapes the ear of the Man on the throne, who only waits to pour out His grace at our faintest call.

> *Where high the heavenly temple stands,*
> *The house of God not made with hands,*
> *A great High Priest our nature wears,*
> *The guardian of mankind appears.*
>
> *He who for men their surety stood,*
> *And poured on earth His precious blood,*
> *Pursues in heaven His mighty plan,*
> *The Savior and the Friend of man.*
>
> *Though now ascended up on high,*
> *He bends on earth a brother's eye;*
> *Partaker of the human name,*
> *He knows the frailty of our frame.*

73

In every pang that rends the heart
The Man of Sorrows had a part;
He sympathizes with our grief,
And to the sufferer sends relief.

With boldness, therefore, at the throne,
Let us make all our sorrows known,
And ask the aid of heavenly power
To help us in the evil hour.[22]

The supreme Gift that the ascended Victor poured out upon men was the Holy Spirit; and by the strength of that Gift His suffering ones may live in triumph today, as God in His sovereignty works to perfect them to His glory. "And I will pray the Father, and he shall give you another Comforter, that he may abide with you for ever," He told His disciples as He prepared them for His departure. "He dwelleth with you, and shall be in you. I will not leave you comfortless: I will come to you." And come He does, in the person of that "other Jesus": speaking peace to our troubled hearts; hushing our fears; bringing forth His own fruit from the sharply pruned branches of our lives; teaching us to abide in Him and His love; showing us the wonders of answered prayer; giving His joy in the midst of our pain; calling us His friends; and making us witnesses to His risen Life, even within the confines of the hedges wherein He has placed us. *(John 14:16-18)*

And all the while the mighty Spirit, working in us by His power, is perfecting us to do God's will, working in us that which is pleasing in His sight until we come to the measure of the stature of the fullness of Christ. *(Eph. 4:13)*

Is any price too high to pay for the privilege of knowing Jesus Christ, of entering, in however small a measure, into the fellowship of His sufferings, of learning to live by the power of His resurrection, of being perfected and prepared to serve Him in the glory of heaven? His promises and His faithfulness are ours to live by within the strictures of His hedges.

74

Work on, then, Lord, till on my soul
  Eternal light shall break,
And in Thy likeness perfected,
  I satisfied shall wake![23]

WHY?

'Lord, if I love Thee and Thou lovest me,
   Why need I any more these toilsome days?
Why should I not run singing up Thy ways
   Straight into heaven, to rest myself with Thee?
What need remains of death-pangs yet to be,
   If all my soul is quickened in Thy praise?
If all my heart loves Thee, what need the amaze,
   Struggle and dimness of an agony?'

'Bride whom I love, if thou too lovest Me,
   Thou needs must choose My likeness for thy dower:
So wilt Thou toil in patience, and abide
   Hungering and thirsting for that blessed hour
When I My likeness shall behold in thee,
   And thou therein shalt waken satisfied.'[18]

11

CHOSEN

He hath chosen us in him before the foundation of the world, that we should be holy and without blame before him in love . . . in whom also we have obtained an inheritance . . . that we should be to the praise of his glory. (Eph. 1:4, 11, 12)

The God of our father hath chosen thee, that thou shouldest know his will, and see that Just One, and shouldest hear the voice of his mouth. For thou shalt be his witness unto all men of what thou hast seen and heard. (Acts 22:14, 15)

All who know Christ as Savior are His chosen ones, and high is the destiny to which we have been called. We are chosen to be holy before God and man and to live in such a way that our lives will call forth praise to Him. We are chosen to know God's will, to see His face and hear His voice, and to be witnesses before earth and hell and heaven to the reality and strength of the life of God in the soul of man.

God's reasons for choosing us lie hidden in the inscrutability of His sovereignty. He chose the Israelites not for any virtue of their own, but simply because He loved them; and He chooses us despite our reluctance to be His: "Ye have not chosen me, but I have chosen you." He does not choose many who are wise or mighty or noble, but rather chooses the foolish, weak, and despised of earth to bring to nothing the world's wisdom, that the glory of redemption may be seen to belong not to man, but to God alone. (Deut. 7:6-8; John 15:16; 1 Cor. 1:26-29)

God has made a covenant with His chosen ones, and for them He purposes only good, promising joy and ultimate triumph. But He also has chosen us for service: "The Lord hath chosen you to stand before him, to serve him, and that ye should minister unto him." He has chosen us to be good soldiers in the invisible war and to bring forth fruit that will endure throughout eternity. For each of His chosen, God has His own particular place and purpose. (Pss. 89:3; 105:43; Rev. 17:14; 2 Chron. 29:11; 2 Tim. 2:3-4; John 15:16)

And to some of His loved ones He whispers gently, "Behold, I have chosen thee in the furnace of affliction"; then tenderly He places about them one of His restricting hedges. "Thou art my servant whom I have chosen," He tells us, and asks us to serve Him in the crucible of pain. (Isa. 48:10; 41:9)

When God sent Ananias to release the newly converted Saul from his blindness, He disclosed His purpose for Saul's life, and a strange and difficult purpose it was: "He is a chosen vessel unto me, to bear my name before the Gentiles, and kings, and the children of Israel. For I will shew him how great things he must suffer for my name's sake." Chosen to suffer! To serve Him, yes; to praise Him, yes; but to suffer for Him? How strange seems such a choice! (Acts 9:15-16)

If God has chosen us to suffer for Him, can we say to Him from a heart rich in faith, "Blessed is the man whom thou choosest . . . we shall be satisfied with the goodness of thy house, even of thy holy temple," even when we know that that temple must be a hedge of pain? (Ps. 65:4)

Suffering chosen and sent by God can be a privilege—perhaps one which none would choose for himself, but the true

78

heart will not refuse it. Listen to a man of God writing about God-given suffering:

When Paul wrote Philippians, he was a prisoner in Rome. Four times in chapter 1 he speaks of "my bonds" (vv. 7, 13, 14, 16). Yet this is the epistle of joy. . . . And nowhere does Paul rise higher than in this word: ". . . it hath been granted in the behalf of Christ . . . to suffer" (1:29, ASV). Think of it! He is telling us that it is a privilege to suffer for the Lord, a favor granted, a gift of grace! How can it be?

We can rejoice in suffering for the name of the Savior because such experiences have the potential of making us stronger spiritually. Paul's sufferings, he said, "shall turn to my salvation" (1:19) . . . In the alchemy of God, trials can be stepping-stones to spiritual maturity. The meaning of testing is not merely in proving our strength, but in increasing it.

We can rejoice in suffering for the name of the Savior because God can make such an experience a testimony that speaks to those who do not know Him. Listen to Paul: "the things which have happened unto me have fallen out rather unto the furtherance of the gospel" (1:12).

We can rejoice in suffering for the name of the Savior because the end result, when patiently and victoriously borne, is the glory of God. "Christ shall be magnified in my body" (v. 20). What a privilege! Suffering for Christ's sake can be used to exalt, to glorify, to praise, to extol the Savior. He is shown to be great through us! For He is the answer to our need for courage, for endurance, for strength. No light privilege this, to bring glory to the Son of God—now and forever.

Write it large upon your heart, child of God through faith in the Savior: "to you it hath been granted . . . to suffer."[25]

79

All the promises of God are for all His people; yet special promises seem to fit special needs. If God has chosen you to suffer, He has many a word that is spoken particularly for you.

> Therefore, all the comforts, promises, and mercies God offereth to the afflicted, they are as so many love-letters written to you. Take them to you, and claim your right, and be not robbed. It is no small comfort that God hath written some scriptures to you which He hath not written to others. . . . Your God is like a friend that sendeth a letter to a whole house and family, but speaketh in His letter to some by name, that are dearest to Him in the house.[17]

Words that may have special significance to those whom God has hedged about with suffering are those in which He speaks of having chosen His people to be His inheritance. God, who could have chosen anything He wished for His inheritance, who, indeed, had no need to choose any inheritance at all since all things were already His, has chosen in infinite love and condescension to have His inheritance in His saints. Blessed are the people whom He has chosen for His own inheritance! (Deut. 4:20; 32:9; Eph. 1:18)

Moreover, He has said that He Himself will be the inheritance of His people, and this can be precious to those whom He has chosen to offer up to Him the spiritual sacrifices of sorrow or pain. Much that He gives to others must be denied you: not for you is the busy life of active service, the victor's shout after the heat of battle. But He speaks with particular tenderness to you when He says, "Thou shalt have no inheritance in their land, neither shalt thou have any part among them: I am thy part and thine inheritance." (Num. 18:20)

Shall we not, then, look up in love and trust and answer with the psalmist: "The Lord is the portion of mine inheritance and of my cup: thou maintainest my lot. The lines are fallen unto me in pleasant places; yea, I have a goodly heritage. (Ps. 16:5-6)

Only if we can learn to look upon our trials as having been chosen for us by the One who has made us to be His own inheritance and who has given Himself to us as our portion and inheritance in return, can we stand up to the pressures of pain and trouble with unbroken spirit and bring forth from our thorny walls the fruit which He requires of us.

> As long as we want to be different from what God wants us to be at the time, we are only tormenting ourselves to no purpose.[6]

Only in acceptance can we find peace. Is it so difficult to accept the portion He has chosen for us when He gives us Himself? Let us bring our wills to Him to be molded to His own and strive to say:

> Let Him make of me what He pleaseth, if He make salvation out of it to me. . . . It is good, Lord Jesus, because Thou hast done it.[17]

He who is able to bring forth rose from brier is able to make the thorn of your hedge blossom and bring forth fruit. Will you deliberately rejoice in His choice for you, lay hold upon God as your special portion and inheritance, and let Him transform your hedge into a thing of beauty and fruitfulness?

O FOR A HEART TO PRAISE MY GOD

O for a heart to praise my God!
   A heart from sin set free;
A heart that always feels Thy blood,
   So freely shed for me;

A heart resigned, submissive, meek,
   My great Redeemer's throne,
Where only Christ is heard to speak,
   Where Jesus reigns alone;

A humble, lowly, contrite heart,
   Believing, true and clean,
Which neither life nor death can part
   From Him that dwells therein;

A heart in every thought renewed,
   And full of love divine,
Perfect, and right, and pure, and good—
   A copy, Lord, of Thine!

Thy nature, gracious Lord, impart:
   Come quickly from above;
Write Thy new Name upon my heart,
   Thy new, best Name of Love![45]

12

PARTAKERS

God has a glorious destiny prepared for His chosen ones, and that inheritance is ours to be used and enjoyed not only in heaven, but here and now. Those whom God has hedged about, in particular, might well meditate deeply upon His purposes for His people; for while they hold much of suffering, they hold more of glory.

"Christ is seldom a reality unless He is first a necessity," someone has aptly remarked.[8] Perhaps the necessities of your hedged-in life, great and pressing as they are, may serve to make the realities of your glorious destiny a greater strength to live by than if you knew no such restrictions.

God in Christ has made us to be partakers of all that He is and has, and in turn has Himself become to the fullest extent a partaker of our humanity. In this double partaking, ourselves of God and God of us, we may find strength and grace for our every need. Let us look at some of the riches of our possessions in Him.

God has made us to be partakers of the heavenly calling, partakers of Christ, partakers of the Holy Ghost, and partakers of the divine nature. Thus He has made us to be one with God Himself, and we have all the resources of the Godhead at our disposal to meet our needs. If "peace is the possession of adequate resources," as someone has defined it,[8] why should we ever be in disquiet? *(Heb. 3:1, 14; 6:4; 2 Pet. 1:4)*

But we have also been made one with the community of believers, the Church universal, so that we have the resources of communal fellowship as well; for He has made us partakers of the inheritance of the saints in light. We are made partakers of the Gospel and of grace. We are partakers of the Lord's table and of the blood and body of Christ. Thus we are made one with the whole worshiping, suffering, triumphing Church of Christ and can draw upon that blessed community for grace and strength. *(Col. 1:12; 1 Cor. 9:23; Phil. 1:7; 1 Cor. 10:21, 16, 17)*

We are given the promise of sharing in a certain harvest and are told that we shall be partakers of the fruits. But we are warned that we are also to be partakers of the afflictions of the gospel. The writer to the Hebrews makes it clear that no true son of the Father will be left without chastisement, whereof all are partakers; but he goes on to disclose the reason for such suffering: it is that we might be partakers of His holiness. *(2 Tim. 2:6; 1:8; Heb. 12:8, 10)*

What high and holy calling is here! Is any price too great to pay for such an eternal end?

"As ye are partakers of the sufferings, so shall ye be also of the consolation," Paul assures us. Peter has the same message: "Think it not strange concerning the fiery trial which is to try you, as though some strange thing happened unto you: but rejoice, inasmuch as ye are partakers of Christ's sufferings; that, when his glory shall be revealed, ye may be glad also with exceeding joy." And Peter goes on to say that as "a witness of the sufferings of Christ," he is "also a partaker of the glory that shall be revealed." *(2 Cor. 1:7; 1 Pet. 4:12-13; 5:1)*

So the purpose of our suffering is plain: its end is glory and likeness to Jesus Christ. Shall those who suffer most share most richly in that glory and perfection? We cannot tell. But if there is one thing that pain, rightly used, will do for us, it is to increase our capacity for God; and the greater our capacity for Him, the more fully we shall be filled with Him, and surely the more greatly we shall one day "glorify God and enjoy Him forever."[28]

> *If pain be the hardest ill of all*
> *For mortal flesh and heart to bear in peace,*
> *It is the one comes straightest from God's hand,*
> *And makes us feel Him nearest to ourselves.*
>
> *God gives us light and love, and all good things*
> *Richly for joy, and power, to use aright;*
> *But then we may forget Him in His gifts:—*
> *We cannot well forget the hand that holds*
> *And pierces us, and will not let us go.*[24]

The Savior asks His children to undergo nothing that He Himself has not first sounded to its depths. Since all mortal ills are the result of death, and sickness and pain are actually a slow form of death, this means that the Lord Jesus not only partook of them for and with us, but is able to deliver us from the power of this death of which we must daily partake. He has become our merciful and faithful High Priest, able to succor His own because of His full and intimate partaking of our humanity and our death.

Nor has the Savior left us without knowledge of how we may grasp the grace He so freely offers. He has given unto us exceeding great and precious promises: that *by these* we might be partakers of the divine nature. It is as we learn to lay His Word on our hearts and make it our own, that gradually, imperceptibly, we become true partakers of His nature, His holiness, His glory. (2 Pet. 1:4)

Such learning is not the work of a moment; indeed, as Rutherford puts it, "Ye must go in at heaven's gates, and your book in your hand, still learning."[17] And we learn by hearing and by taking unto ourselves all God's promises.

Shall we not, then, seek to learn all the lessons that God has hidden for us within our hedges? Let us not lose our opportunity to be made partakers of His very self. Let us strive to grow up in Him unto maturity.

God has nothing but good to teach us, no matter how great the afflictions through which His lessons may come. Of the shining list of gifts of which He has made us to be partakers, sixteen are glories, while only three—Christ's sufferings, the afflictions of the Gospel, and chastisement—entail anything of pain. Shall we shrink from such a cup of blessing offered us by our Father's hand?

> Drink then to the very dregs the cup handed to you by no enemy and no stranger, but by your Father. . . . God never deprives us of something, be it temporal or spiritual, except to impart Himself in His very essence, after we have had the necessary preparation.[6]

IN DARKNESS

In faithfulness hast Thou afflicted me,
      O Sovereign Love;
I will not fear, but look in faith to Thee
      Enthroned above,
And know my Father's heart of grace has planned
This darkness that I cannot understand.

I rest in Thee, though human tears may fall
      In sorrow's hour;
Upon Thy faithfulness I cast my all,
      And claim Thy power
To work eternal wealth of holy gain
From this deep night of loneliness and pain.

In faithfulness hast Thou afflicted me,
      Most gracious One;
In faithfulness may I accept from Thee
      This Thou hast done;
For Thou Thy gifts of darkness dost impart
But to disclose the fullness of Thy heart.[1]

13

IN DARKNESS

Despite our growing knowledge of God's sovereign purposes for us in pain, and the gradually increasing spiritual strength we can learn to realize from the contemplation of our riches in Christ Jesus and the glorious destiny He has prepared for us—a destiny for which our sufferings even now are shaping us, and to which they may in no small measure contribute—as long as we are in this body we shall be subject to periods of darkness, doubt, depression, even despair. "He hath fenced up my way that I cannot pass, and he hath set darkness in my paths"; "He hath brought me into darkness, but not into light": so Job and Jeremiah mourned the darkness that so often has been the lot of God's servants. (*Job* 19:8; *Lam.* 3:2)

Darkness and difficulty are bound to be part of the hedge with which God has enclosed those who must suffer, but we must learn not to be dismayed in the face of darkness. When light seems to be denied us so that we find ourselves crying out with the writer of Psalm 77, "Hath God forgotten to be gracious?", we must learn to follow through to his conclusion: "*This is my infirmity*"; and then to his solution: "*I will* remember the years of the right hand of the most High. *I will remember* the works of the Lord: surely *I will remember* thy wonders of old. *I will meditate* also of all thy work, and *talk of thy doings.*" The psalmist realized that his apparent darkness really lay in his own infirmity, not in his God, and that it could only be dissipated through the deliberate raising of a memorial to remembered Light by setting himself to remember the Lord, to meditate on Him, and to talk about His mercies. When we discipline ourselves to follow a similar path, we, too, shall be able to exclaim in joy with the psalmist, "How great thou art!" *(Ps. 77:9-13)*

What is infirmity? Infirmity for the Christian has been described as those avenues in his nature or his circumstances through which temptation, which could lead to sin, can most easily gain access to the citadel of his soul. The identification and understanding of individual infirmities, followed by the setting of specific and adequate spiritual guardians at each gateway, are the particular tasks of all who would know Christian maturity. For the sufferer, such maturity is essential to survival. A hedge of pain or grief is a formidable infirmity indeed, and those who must live therein must learn to cope with the peculiar difficulties and darkness that it entails.

Two of the hardest things a sufferer must learn to live with and to overcome are the loneliness and misunderstanding that spring from his pain, whatever form it may take, and which are sometimes harder to bear than the actual suffering itself. He is lonely because he is often shut off in a physical sense from other people; but he also is lonely, and perhaps this is the more penetrating loneliness, because no other person, not even in the closest bond of love or friendship, can fully enter into those sealed places where the human spirit must suffer. Misunderstanding will meet the sufferer on all sides, for if even his nearest and dearest cannot fully comprehend his needs, then others will not even try to understand him, and this can be anguish to a sensitive soul.

Other peculiar difficulties caused by illness or stress lie closer to home: an inability to concentrate for even a few minutes; wandering thoughts that make it almost impossible to repeat even a single verse of Scripture in its entirety and equally impossible to pray in any sustained way; nervous tension that holds one in an iron grip from which there seems to be no release; a predisposition to depression and fear; the lethargy that may accompany the constant taking of required medication; the inability to maintain a consistent devotional time because of the vagaries of pain.

In league with these enemies in their effort to storm the city of Mansoul are the frustration and the sense of uselessness that are the inevitable lot of those who are forced to live out their years in the backwater of life while its mainstream forever passes them by. All these things are certainly infirmities—avenues along which the temptation to sin will daily, hourly, momentarily be seeking to gain entry; and every form of suffering has its own particular list of attendant sorrows. How can we learn to withstand such crushing adversaries of the human spirit?

Let us turn again to Psalm 77. "I will remember," the psalmist began. We must remember that we do not stand alone against our infirmities: they are not only known to God, but He has made more than adequate provision for them. He has given the Holy Spirit to help our infirmities, and He ceaselessly makes intercession for us according to the will of God. The Lord Jesus knows the full power of our infirmities, for He took them upon Himself, and now stands at the right hand of the Father praying for us. (Rom. 8:26-27; Heb. 4:15; Matt. 8:17)

We must remember God in all His attributes, both human and divine, as revealed to us in His Word, His world, and His working in history, in the lives of His saints universal, in the lives of our friends, and in our own lives. We must learn to do this in the face of fear and failure, of depression and discouragement, when we feel utterly alone in the darkness, afar from God and estranged from all humanity. When racking pain, numbing weakness, or overwhelming sorrow blots into oblivion our physical ability to remember, we must learn to rest upon the truth of God's remembered mercies, even though we are totally unable to bring them to specific recall. We must remember Jesus Christ; and as we seek to stay our souls upon Him, we will find that, although in ourselves we are insufficient for these things, our sufficiency is of God. "He remembered . . . . they remembered not," the psalmist wrote of God's dealings with Israel, and God is the same today. Not only does He *know* the terrible necessities and the awful limitations of our poor human hearts, minds, and bodies, and the extremities of our pain, but He *remembers* them: "He knoweth our frame; he remembereth that we are dust." (2 Cor. 2:16; 3:5; Ps. 78:39, 42; Ps. 103:14)

So we must set ourselves deliberately to remember Him, to meditate upon Him, and to talk of His doings. If necessary, we must count upon His unfelt and unremembered mercies; and if even that should prove impossible at times, we must simply rest upon the fact that He will never for one instant forget us: He knows, and He remembers. Whether we feel it or not, we have His presence for our loneliness; His understanding for the human misunderstanding that so ruthlessly assaults our quivering sensitivities; His unchanging and unchangeable purpose for the seeming hopelessness of our frustration and apparent uselessness; His strength to be made perfect in our weakness of thinking, praying, reading His Word, even remembering Him; His grace to be sufficient for all our needs. Our very infirmities can make the power of Christ rest more fully upon us.

"For this we have Jesus"[29] must be the anchor to which we cling as we do battle with the powers of darkness, even when we are engulfed by darkness so deep that it robs us of all sense of His presence. "I am the light of the world," He has told us. "He that followeth me shall not walk in darkness, but shall have the light of life." The Prince of Darkness may seek to overcome us, but God is in control of the darkness He allows to come to His children. "The light shined in darkness, and the darkness could not put it out," wrote John of the coming of the Savior, and such is the experience of every soul that truly trusts Him, no matter how dark the night may be. (John 8:12; 1:5)

Although we may experience darkness, we are not under its power, for God, who has delivered us from the power of darkness, has promised to bring us safely through it. "When I sit in darkness, the Lord shall be a light unto me," wrote Micah, and Job recorded: "His candle shined upon my head, and . . . by his light I walked through darkness." (Col. 1:13; Micah 7:8; Job 29:3)

God can bring good from our darkness. "I will give thee the treasures of darkness, and hidden riches of secret places," He has promised, and through us He will speak His comforts to others: "What I tell you in darkness, that speak ye in light," said the Lord Jesus. (Isa. 45:3; Matt. 10:27)

We must learn to suffer in darkness if we are called to suffer for God's glory and truly want to realize the fullness of His purposes for us, for we walk by faith, not by sight. (2 Cor. 5:7)

> Therefore gird up thyself, and come, to stand
> Unflinching under the unfaltering hand
> That waits to prove thee to the uttermost.
> It were not hard to suffer by the hand
> If thou couldst see His face—but in the dark!
> That is the one last trial: be it so.
> Christ was forsaken, so must thou be too:
> How couldst thou suffer but in seeming, else?
> Thou wilt not see the face nor feel the hand,
> Only the cruel crushing of the feet
> When through the bitter night the Lord comes down
> To tread the winepress. Not by sight, but faith:
> Endure, endure: be faithful to the end![24]

HE KEEPETH COVENANT

Jehovah God thy Keeper is:
    His Father-heart is watching o'er thee;
No wit, no skill, no care like His:
    His love prepares thy way before thee;
And changeless as the eternal Throne,
He keepeth covenant with His own.

His purposes unfailing stand—
    What canst thou need, and He deny thee?
The worlds sustain at His command—
    Strength for thy day will He supply thee.
His hand will feed thee, come what may:
He keepeth covenant day by day.

The covering wings of God are wide—
    Those faithful wings about thee hover,
Guard thee from ill on every side,
    With everlasting mercies cover.
His rainbow in thy cloud appears:
He keepeth covenant through the years.

Eternal as His Throne above,
    His word to thee cannot be broken;
He loves thee with undying love—
    His hands, His feet, His side, the token.
Thy Father-God, thy Savior-Friend,
He keepeth covenant to the end.

Moment by moment, in His power
    The trusting soul is kept forever;
He keepeth covenant hour by hour:
    Nor life nor death His faith can sever,
But, until shines His perfect day,
He keepeth covenant all the way.[1]

14

CLOUD AND COVENANT

"He is God, the faithful God, which keepeth covenant and mercy with them that love him." (Deut. 7:9)

When God led His people out of Egypt to bring them into the land He had covenanted to Abraham, Isaac, and Jacob, He led them by a pillar of cloud and fire. No ordinary cloud was this, but the very presence of Jehovah Himself, for we read: "And the Lord went before them by day in a pillar of a cloud, to lead them the way; and by night in a pillar of fire, to give them light." Although the cloud was darkness to Israel's enemies, it gave protection, guidance, light, and heat to God's chosen people. *(Exod. 13:21)*

Many times God drew near to His people in a cloud. When He gave them bread from heaven in the wilderness, His glory appeared in the cloud; when the law was given at Sinai, a cloud covered the mount; and when, after Israel's sin, the law was given a second time, the Lord descended in a cloud to renew His covenant with His repentant people. And it was after his experience in the cloud with God that Moses' face shone with God's glory. *(Exod. 16:10; 24: 15, 18; 34:5, 29)*

95

Again, when Moses had finished preparing the Tabernacle, a cloud covered it, and the glory of the Lord filled the tabernacle. The Shekinah dwelt in the Holy of Holies where God had promised to appear in the cloud upon the mercy seat. And when the Ark of the covenant was brought up to Solomon's temple, the cloud filled the house of the Lord, so that the priests could not stand to minister because of the cloud: for the glory of the Lord had filled the house of the Lord. (Exod. 40:34; 1 Kings 8:10-11)

Nor did the cloud cease to signify God's presence in the New Testament. When the Father saluted His Son on the Mount of Transfiguration, it was from within the brightness of an overshadowing cloud. When, His work of redemption accomplished, the risen Savior ascended into His glory, a cloud received Him out of their sight. And in teaching His friends about His final revelation as King in the end of the age, Jesus stated that He would come in a cloud with power and great glory. (Matt. 17:5; Acts 1:9; Luke 21:27)

When the great Jehovah first spread a cloud for a covering and fire to give light in the night, it was in fulfillment of His covenant with His people. And so it is today. Our God is still the God of the covenant, and it is within the confines of His covenant mercies that His children experience His presence in cloud and fire. (Ps. 105:39)

> Round each habitation hovering,
> See! the cloud and fire appear,
> For a glory and a covering,
> Showing that the Lord is near.[47]

Often the ways of God are shrouded in mystery. The dark "cloud of unknowing,"[30] even of seeming separation from Himself, and the fire of the furnace of affliction may be yours; but as the cloud concealed the presence of Jehovah Himself, and the fire both protected His people from their enemies and illumined their way, so it is now. And no matter how barren our experience of God may be at any particular time, or how prone we may be to forget His promises, He will ever be mindful of His covenant. In His own good time He will make darkness light, for the secret of the Lord is with them that fear Him; and He will show them His covenant. *(Pss. 111:5; 25:14)*

God's covenant with His children is an everlasting covenant. It is a covenant of mercy and of peace. Its mediator is none other than the eternal Son of God who sealed it with His own blood. In fact, the Savior *is* God's covenant with His people, for the Spirit through Isaiah wrote of His suffering servant in these words: "I the Lord ... will ... give thee for a covenant of the people, for a light of the Gentiles; to open the blind eyes, to bring out the prisoners from the prison, and them that sit in darkness out of the prison house." No wonder that ours is a covenant-keeping God! *(2 Sam 23:5; Heb. 13:20; Isa. 55:3; Num. 25:12; Heb. 12:24; 13:20; Isa. 42:6-7)*

And covenant-keeping he is indeed. "The Lord thy God, he is God, the faithful God, which keepeth covenant and mercy with them that love him and keep his commandments to a thousand generations," He has declared. "For the mountains shall depart, and the hills be removed; but my kindness shall not depart from thee; neither shall the covenant of my peace be removed, saith the Lord." And this God has told us that we are the children of the covenant. What a refuge in which to trust in the midst of our cloud and fire! *(Deut. 7:9; Isa. 54: 10; Acts 3:25)*

When God established His covenant with Noah following the Flood, He gave a token to serve as a perpetual reminder of His promise to mankind. Was it by accident that the token of covenant was a rainbow shining in a cloud?

Does the eternal God need a reminder lest He should forget His word? No, but man does; and here the gracious Father speaks in the language of His human family. The cloud He here designates to bear His token is not that of the Shekinah so often used in Scripture, but merely an earthly storm cloud; yet even that He touches with His glory.

The rainbow is mentioned in only three other places in the Bible, and in each of them it speaks of the presence of the living God ruling the universe from His eternal Throne. Ezekiel's vision concluded with a glimpse of "a man above" seated upon the throne, and "as the appearance of the bow that is in the cloud in the day of rain, so was the appearance of the brightness round about. This was the appearance of the likeness of the glory of the Lord." John, in his apocalyptic vision, gazed upon the same dazzling sight: "Behold, a throne was set in heaven, and one sat on the throne. . . . and there was a rainbow round about the throne." Later, when he was shown God's messenger, the mighty angel with the little book, he, too, was "clothed with a cloud: and a rainbow was upon his head" as he carried out his share in God's work. (Ezek. 1:26, 28; Rev. 4:2-3; 10:1)

Is it so difficult to live a life hedged in by clouds when the covenant token that God has placed in them is a part of the rainbow which encircles His eternal Throne? As we look up at the desolate clouds that shadow our lonely lives, searching out His rainbow, we discover the presence of our sovereign God Himself, for He has promised that He waits for us there. And if there were no cloud, how should we know his rainbow?

It is an awesome and exciting experience, when traveling by plane on a day so overcast that nothing but cloud is visible in every direction, suddenly to rise above the grey and emerge into sunlight so brilliant that even the dark bank of cloud that blots out all view of earth is aglow with the glory of the sun. Our covenant-keeping God can so transfigure the clouds that hedge in our lives if we will seek Him there.

Clouds have many uses in our natural universe. A world without clouds would be a world without rain, unshaded from the burning sun, hence without water, vegetation, or life. Our lives, too, would wither without clouds. Is it without design that the great Creator has planned that clouds shall form part of every life—even that some of His chosen ones shall know little else but clouds? How, otherwise, could eternal fruition be brought about? Will those who know most of His clouds know most of fruition, know most of His presence, know most purely the glory of His covenant token? None can say; but it is certain that they will have all that they need, all that they can contain. So we accept His clouds as our highest good, knowing that He sends them and that He dwells within them with us, even though we may not always be conscious of His presence.

Samuel Rutherford, whose writings about the person of the Savior are among the most intimate and fragrant Christian expressions of all time, was a man who experienced many periods of darkness when Christ seemed to withdraw His presence from him. His letters contain many plaintive passages where he comments on the subject. But he also saw the true meaning of such darkness in the life of a Christian.

> *I think that absence of His sweet presence is Christ's trying of us, not simply our sin against Him. . . . Sometimes Christ hath an errand elsewhere, for mere trial; and then, though ye gave Him king's cheer, He will away; as is clear in desertions for mere trial and not for sin. . . . His art, His shining wisdom, His beauty, speak loudest in blackness, weakness, deadness. . . . And blessed be God, that after a low ebb and so sad a word, "Lord Jesus, it is long since I saw Thee," that even then our wings are growing, and the absence of sweet Jesus breedeth a new fleece of desires and longing for Him.[17]*

If you have never covenanted with God for His fullness of Covenant blessing in your clouded life, why not do so now? You are His; you have accepted the hedge, the cloud, He has given. But if you have never actually claimed the fellowship of His presence not only in spite of your cloud, but in it and because of it, you have missed some of the richness that He has planned for you and ardently longs to bestow.

PRAYER

Prayer is the soul's sincere desire,
    Uttered or unexpressed;
The motion of a hidden fire
    That trembles in the breast.

Prayer is the burden of a sigh,
    The falling of a tear,
The upward glancing of an eye,
    When none but God is near.

Prayer is the simplest form of speech
    That infant lips can try;
Prayer the sublimest strains that reach
    The Majesty on high.

Prayer is the contrite sinner's voice
    Returning from his ways,
While angels in their songs rejoice
    And cry, "Behold, he prays."

Prayer is the Christian's vital breath,
    The Christian's native air,
His watchword at the gates of death:
    He enters heaven with prayer.

O Thou by whom we come to God,
    The Life, the Truth, the Way!
The path of prayer Thyself hast trod:
    Lord, teach us how to pray![33]

15

WHEN YOU CAN'T PRAY

So God's hedge has closed about you on all sides, and the skies are black above you. All sense of God's presence seems to have left you, and, try as you will, you can't pray.

How well you know that you never stood in greater need of fellowship with God in prayer! But it seems impossible; you just cannot summon up enough physical strength or mental energy to really pray. Another aching, sleepless night or a night of watching by a suffering loved one; another morning of awakening to a world bounded on every side by pain or nausea, or both; another day or week or month of such utter nervous exhaustion and inability to concentrate that you are completely unable to gather the shreds of your shattered personality and your unspeakable need and bring them to the Throne—by some such hopeless situation you are thwarted in your every attempt to reach out to God, your only Source of supply. How can anyone find grace to help in face of need like this?

The first thing we must realize is that it is neglect of prayer or refusal to pray that is sin, not the inability to pray. The prayer difficulties so frequently experienced by sufferers might rather be classed as infirmity and are usually an integral part of the particular problem that constitutes God's hedge for them. Especially is this true if we must endure prolonged physical pain or weakness, when our infirmity is literally physical infirmity. If the earnest desire to pray is present, we must not condemn ourselves because we find prayer hard or even impossible.

"Lord, all my desire is before thee; and my groaning is not hid from thee," we may cry; "the desire of our soul is to thy name, and to the remembrance of thee." If this is really true, then it will also be true that "He will fulfil the desire of them that fear him." (Ps. 38:9; Isa. 26:8; Ps. 145:19)

However, before we can claim such a promise, we must be quite sure of two things. First, we must entertain no controversy with God or our prayers will most certainly be hindered. Second, we must wage a never-ceasing warfare against allowing our infirmity, whatever it may be, to gain the place of power in our lives and so to come between us and the Lord. Even those who have resisted Satan valiantly in this regard for many years know that it is all too easy to simply give in to a situation that seems to be both permanent and hopeless and to cease to strive for anything in the nature of serious prayer. But for those who maintain constant vigilance on these two points, God has His own ways of reaching out to those who have valid difficulty in reaching out to Him. "The Lord is nigh unto all them that call upon him, to all that call upon him in truth." (Ps. 145:18)

What a comfort and blessing to know that it is God's faithfulness by which we stand and upon which we rest—not our own works, even the right and necessary work of prayer! "Thy mercy, O Lord, is in the heavens; and thy faithfulness reacheth unto the clouds," even the clouds that darken above our thorny hedge. And God has made adequate provision for all our needs, even for this strange necessity, the inability to pray. (Ps. 36:5)

At the right hand of the throne of God, Jesus stands on our

behalf, our great High Priest. Touched with the feeling of our infirmities, He prays for us in the power of His endless life with perfect, holy, all-prevailing prayer, whether we are able to pray for ourselves or not. And this strength is ours, even when we may have no sense at all of its reality. (Heb. 8:1; 4:15; 7:16)

And as if that were not enough, God in the abundance of His grace has made further provision for our need. The Spirit of God Himself, even the mighty Comforter, gift of the ascended Savior to His own, also helps our infirmities by pouring Himself out for us in ceaseless prayer. He who searches the hearts of men and knows what is the mind of God for us makes intercession for us according to the will of God. (Rom. 8:26-27)

And so the weakest believer, consciously or unconsciously, is caught up in the eternal triangle of prayer: his own feeble groanings are made one with the holy prayers of the Savior for him and with the prayers of the all-powerful, all-knowing Spirit within him. And all this is true and is working on our behalf even when we feel, like Jeremiah, "He hath set me in dark places . . . he hath hedged me about, that I cannot get out: he hath made my chain heavy. Also when I cry and shout, he shutteth out my prayer. He hath enclosed my ways with hewn stone, he hath made my paths crooked. . . . Thou hast covered thyself with a cloud, that our prayers should not pass through." What a refuge for the hapless, helpless soul! (Lam. 3:6-9; 44)

Though we may be unable to pray as we would wish, there are ways by which we may reach out to God even in our weakness, and we must learn to cultivate them.

We can bring our fragmented minds and lack of ability to concentrate to God and implore Him, "Unite my heart to fear thy name," and then trust Him to do it whether we feel any different or not. We can bring before Him the restless minds and wandering thoughts that plague us and ask Him to stay them upon Himself, claiming His promise that if we commit our works to Him our thoughts will be established. Even if we seem to experience little conscious improvement in our ability to concentrate, by deliberately and regularly placing this problem in His hand we will know an inner growth and health, as in the multitude of our crowding thoughts within us we find that His comforts delight our souls. Let us never cease to ask Him to work this miracle within us. *(Ps. 86:11; Prov. 16:3; Ps. 84:19)*

We can cry unto God. The Scriptures are vocal with the cries of God's suffering saints and bright with the glory of the deliverances that He worked for them. And even now the eyes of the Lord are upon the righteous and His ears are open to their cry. He hears the cry of the afflicted and does not forget the cry of the humble. If all we are able to bring to God is a cry, then let us bring it unceasingly, in faith, and know that He hears us. Our trusting souls will exult with David, "This poor man cried, and the Lord heard him, and saved him out of all his troubles. . . . O taste and see that the Lord is good: blessed is the man that trusteth in him." *(Ps. 34:15; Job 34:28; Pss. 9:12; 34:6,8)*

We can pour out our hearts, our tears, even our complaints before God. "Trust in him at all times," He has told us: "Ye people, pour out your heart before him: God is a refuge for us." *(Ps. 62:8)*

Often such outpourings result in a greater understanding of the nature and purposes of God, with all the succor that such insights bring. Job vigorously protested God's ways with him, his eyes pouring out tears as his heart poured out its complaints to God; yet it was to Job that God gave the beatific vision of life in His presence after death, in an age when death was commonly considered to end all. It was when one despairing psalmist cried to the Lord, "I am so troubled that I cannot speak," that he was enabled to think upon God until he could exclaim in joy, "Who is so great a God as our God? Thou art the God that doest wonders"; and it was after another had poured out his soul in tears to God that he was enabled to utter the sublime affirmation of faith: "Why art thou cast down, O my soul? and why art thou disquieted in me? hope thou in God: for I shall yet praise him for the help of his countenance." And it was after Hannah had poured out her soul before the Lord with such intensity that the child Samuel was given. (*Job* 3:23-24; 16:20; *Pss.* 77:4, 13-14; 42:5; 1 *Sam.* 1:15)

Wordless or fragmented prayers, broken cries, tears, even complaints—God will hear them all. Then let us not fear to come before Him: "Arise, cry out in the night .. pour out thine heart like water before the face of the Lord: lift up thy hands toward him." God in His mercy will accept such prayer. (*Lam.* 2:19)

Our suffering itself may become a form of prayer, if we can learn to let submission and love, even praise, ascend to God through it. It is a wonderful and awesome thing when in the grip of severe pain or sorrow to look up into the face of God and say! "I bring You this—now; accept it for the sake of the Lord Jesus." It may not be the sacrifice we would choose to bring, but if pain is what God has given us, and pain is all we have, we may offer it up to Him as a sacrifice of praise and He will both accept it and hallow it. Such an offering may be one of the purest forms of worship known to the spirit of man.

Above all, we can breathe before God the holy name of Jesus, knowing that nothing is more precious to Him—and that nothing is more feared by the powers of evil—than this strong word. By the strength of that name we can live through hours, days, weeks, even months, years, or a lifetime of pain and sorrow, whether we are able to pray normally or not; by it we can defeat the Tempter who would have us curse God and die. The One who covenanted that He would be a little sanctuary to His dispersed people Israel will Himself become a sanctuary to us in our need. (*Ezek.* 11:16; *Isa.* 8:14)

And always, of course, we will continue to try to pray, whether we feel we are accomplishing anything or not. We will keep regular times for prayer, even though we approach them feeling parched and barren and may have to conclude them feeling the same way. C. S. Lewis once wrote that the cause of evil is never in greater danger than "when a human, no longer desiring, but still intending, to do (God's) will, looks around upon a universe from which every trace of Him seems to have vanished and asks why he has been forsaken and still obeys."[34] I wonder if the prayer situation of a Christian who is seeking to be faithful to God within a hedge of pain may not provide unusually fertile soil for the bringing forth of a special kind of holy and precious spiritual fruit.

And so we continue to come to God in prayer, even though we may have failed so often that we can only cry with the ancient prophet: "O my God, I am ashamed and blush to lift up my face to thee;" for God in His mercy will hear. Our prayer life may be, and probably will be, a fluctuating sort of thing, and we may be tempted to give up, feeling that the Lord is God of the hills but not of the valleys. But God has promised that every valley shall be exalted, and the glory of the Lord shall be revealed; and so we persevere. (Ezra 9:6; 1 Kings 20:28; Isa. 40:4-5)

But we must be patient, for such victories are not won in a day. It was only after Abraham had patiently endured that he obtained the promise, and so it is with us. We must run with patience the race that He sets before us, looking to Jesus, the Author and Finisher of our faith, to perfect His work in us. (Heb. 6:15; 12:1-2)

Faith and patience appear together several times in the New Testament, and we are told that it is through faith and patience that we inherit the promises. We are enjoined to wait patiently for God and to be patient in tribulation; and our patience is marked by God Himself, who says, "I know thy works, and thy labour, and thy patience." (Heb. 6:12; Ps. 37:7; Rom. 12:12; Rev. 2:2)

Such patience is not found in the human heart, but God has made provision for us in this regard, as in all else. By Him we may be "strengthened with all might, according to his glorious

power, *unto all patience and longsuffering with joyfulness.*"
We might think that such magnificent power might be commanded to enable us to go out to conquer the world for the Savior or perform some other task of noble magnitude, but no; it has a mission humbler than that, and one closer to home—that we might be enabled to live in all patience and long-suffering with joyfulness, bringing forth the fruit of holiness unto our God. And one of the difficult things we must learn to overcome by His power is our inability to pray as we know we should. *(Col. 1:11)*

Sometimes when we are too tense or too exhausted to formulate our own prayers, we may find it helpful to pray in the words of others. The Scriptures have sounded the depths of every human need, and in repeating even fragments of God's Word before Him, we are offering true and acceptable prayer. Many excellent books of prayers are available, both ancient and modern, from the sublime *Book of Common Prayer* and other time-proven books to books of prayers in contemporary language. Any or all of these may help us draw near to God. Many of the great hymns of the church can aid us in prayer; there is something about the rhyme, rhythm, and musical setting that makes it easier for some people to remember hymns than to recall passages of scriptural prose, and a few lines of verse will often steal into a mind that is too weary to remember much else. Devotional poems likewise can help clear the thorny pathway to the Throne. Whether the words are our own or those of others it does not matter; they express our need and our desire, and if they will help us to God, let us not hesitate to use them. We should surround ourselves with such helps.

For we are not alone in our problem. Many are the saints who have had to grapple with difficulties in prayer. C.S. Lewis wrote:

> *The worse one is praying, the longer one's prayers take. . . .*
> *I have a notion that what seem our worst prayers may really*

be, in God's eyes, our best. Those, I mean, which are least supported by devotional feeling and contend with the greatest disinclination. For these, perhaps, being nearly all will, come from a deeper level than feeling. In feeling there is so much that is not really ours—so much that comes from weather and health or from the last book read. One thing seems certain. It is no good angling for the rich moments. God sometimes seems to speak to us most intimately when He catches us, as it were, off our guard. Our preparations to receive Him sometimes have the opposite effect. Doesn't Charles Williams say somewhere that "the altar must often be built in one place in order that the fire from heaven may descend somewhere else"?[34]

And listen to Rutherford:

Send a heavy heart up to Christ; it shall be welcome. . . . I shall rather spill twenty prayers than not pray at all. Let my broken words go up to heaven: when they come up into the Great Angel's golden censer, that compassionate Advocate will put together my broken prayers, and perfume them. Words are but the accidents of prayer. . . . Lend Christ your melancholy. Borrow joy and comfort from the Comforter. Bid the Spirit do His office in you; and remember that faith is one thing, and the feeling and notice of faith another.[17]

Tersteegen's letters have much to say on this same subject:

You say you cannot pray. Is there then no Oh and no Ah in your heart? And granted you cannot find even that, when you say you cannot pray, you are praying. . . . Prayer is looking at God, who is ever present, and letting Him look on us. . . . Since you cannot do much to love and praise Him, suffer, as it is given to you from moment to moment, in love and praise to Him.[6]

Juliana of Norwich fought these same battles over six hundred years ago and wrote:

Pray inwardly, though thou think it suits thee not, for it is profitable, though thou feel not, though thou see nought; yea, though thou think thou canst not. For in dryness and in barrenness, in sickness and in feverishness, then in thy prayer well-pleasing to Me, though thou think it suit thee nought but little. And so is all thy believing prayer in My sight. God accepteth the goodwill and travail of His servant, howsoever we feel.[4]

A modern suffering saint, Amy Carmichael, writes of the same battle thus:

When vision fadeth, and the sense of things,
    And powers dissolve like colours in the air,
And no more can I bring Thee offerings,
       Nor any ordered prayer,

Then, like a wind blowing from Paradise,
    Falleth a healing word upon mine ear,
Let the lifting up of my hands be as the evening sacrifice:
       The Lord doth hear.[5]

MAY JESUS CHRIST BE PRAISED

When morning gilds the skies,
My heart, awaking, cries:
   May Jesus Christ be praised!
Alike at work and prayer,
To Jesus I repair:
   May Jesus Christ be praised!

When sleep her balm denies,
My silent spirit sighs:
   May Jesus Christ be praised!
When evil thoughts molest,
With this I shield my breast:
   May Jesus Christ be praised!

Does sadness fill my mind?
A solace here I find:
   May Jesus Christ be praised!
Or fades my earthly bliss?
My comfort still is this:
   May Jesus Christ be praised!

The night becomes as day
When from the heart we say:
   May Jesus Christ be praised!
The pow'rs of darkness fear
When this sweet chant they hear:
   May Jesus Christ be praised!

In heav'n's eternal bliss
The loveliest strain is this:
   May Jesus Christ be praised!
The fairest graces spring
In hearts that ever sing:
   May Jesus Christ be praised!

Be this, while life is mine,
My canticle divine:
   May Jesus Christ be praised!
Be this th'eternal song
Through all the ages long:
   May Jesus Christ be praised![46]

16

PRAISE IS THE ONLY ANSWER

Praise is purer far
  Than any form of prayer;
Prayer climbs the steep ascent to Heaven—
  Praise is already there.[8]

In situations where prayer is exceedingly difficult, even at times impossible, there is one sure means of releasing God's power in our lives if we will use it, and that is praise. It may seem anomalous to suggest that we seek God through praise when we are unable to reach Him through prayer, but this is one of the anomalies of heaven: praise is the only answer.

When Christian, lodging at the Palace Beautiful, was discussing the vicissitudes of the narrow way with his hosts, Prudence asked him:

> *Can you remember by what means you find your annoyances, at times, as if they were vanquished?*

And Christian replied:

> *Yes, when I think what I saw at the cross, that will do it; also when I look upon my broidered coat, that will do it;*

111

*also when I look into the roll that I carry in my bosom,
that will do it; and when my thoughts wax warm about
whither I am going, that will do it.*[9]

There are innumerable things for which even the most
sharply hedged-in Christian can offer praise; things which,
when we think upon them, will enable us, like Christian, to
exclaim, "*That* will do it!"

Praise has been defined as "a confession and due acknowl-
edgement of the great and wonderful excellencies and perfec-
tions that be in God."[13] Praise is far more than mere gratitude: praise is adoration; praise is worship. When we really
take time to think upon our God, how can we do other than
praise Him?

We can praise God for Himself, for what He is: "a Spirit,
infinite, eternal, and unchangeable in his being, wisdom,
power, holiness, justice, goodness and truth."[28] As we seek to
contemplate Him and all the glories of His infinite attributes,
surely the coldest heart cannot but begin to burn within and to
melt before Him in praise.

We can praise Him for His sovereignty, setting a boundary
to our trials that even Satan himself may not pass over: a
sovereignty great enough to turn the tides of history to serve
His own ends; a sovereignty that is in supreme command of
our individual lives; a sovereignty that has power to accomplish all that He decrees. "He doeth according to his will in the
army of heaven, and among the inhabitants of the earth: and
none can stay his hand, or say unto him, What doest thou?"
"When a man's ways please the Lord, he maketh even his
enemies to be at peace with him." "The lot is cast into the lap;
but the whole disposing thereof is of the Lord." "The king's
heart is in the hand of the Lord, as the rivers of water: he
turneth it whithersoever he will." Thus the Spirit of God has
written of God's sovereignty. Should not verses such as these
call forth praise from even the most sharply hedged-in heart?
(Dan. 4:35; Prov. 16:7; 16:33; 21:1)

We can praise God for His faithfulness. Great indeed is His faithfulness, reaching unto the clouds and extending to all generations. "I will not . . . suffer my faithfulness to fail. My covenant will I not break," He has promised. It is in faithfulness that He allows afflictions to come into our lives, and it is this same faithfulness that will not allow us to be tempted beyond measure, but will make a way of escape that we may be able to bear it. Should not the contemplation of such faithfulness fill our hearts with praise? (*Lam.* 3:23; *Pss.* 36:5; 119:90; 89:33-34; 119:75; 1 *Cor.* 10:13)

We can praise God for His wisdom, by which He founded the earth and established the heavens, and by which He plans our lives and overrules in all our circumstances. We can praise Him for the perfection of His ways and that He can make even our hedged-in ways to be perfect. (*Prov.* 3:19; 2 *Sam.* 22:31; *Ps.* 18:32)

We can praise Him for His never-failing mercies and His compassions, which are new every morning. We can praise Him for His past mercies, both to ourselves and to others; for His present mercies, even in our hedged-in circumstances; and for His promise of future mercies. "The future is as bright as the promises of God,"[8] someone has aptly commented; and again, "God is utterly to be trusted."[8] (*Lam.* 3:22-23; 2 *Cor.* 1:10)

His love, His grace, His holiness, His justice, His power— for what can we not praise Him? For all that He is and does, and most of all for the fact that He is ours and we are His, let us think upon our God and cultivate the spirit of praise.

"Whoso offereth praise glorifieth me," He has told us, and this is particularly true when praise must be born out of pain. But is it not to the offering up of acceptable spiritual sacrifices through Christ that we have been called? The Scriptures have much to say about the sacrifice of praise, and praise that ascends to God from an altar of sorrow or suffering is precious and fragrant sacrifice indeed. In seeking to cultivate a spirit of praise we will bring glory to God and find the strength to endure. *(Ps. 50:23; 1 Pet. 2:5; Heb. 13:15)*

It is for God's praise that we were predestinated: "predestinated . . . to the praise of the glory of his grace." It is for God's praise that we were formed: "This people have I formed for myself; they shall shew forth my praise." It is for God's praise that we were chosen: "Ye are a chosen generation . . . that ye should shew forth the praises of him who hath called you out of darkness into his marvellous light." Our very trials are planned for the purpose of praise: "that the trial of your faith, being much more precious than of gold that perisheth, though it be tried with fire, might be found unto praise and honour and glory at the appearing of Jesus Christ." *(Eph. 1:5-6; Isa. 43:21; 1 Pet. 2:9; 1:7)*

Who is sufficient for a destiny like this? Certainly not our poor humanity. But "all God's commands are enablings,"[8] and God Himself has promised to be our praise. The Lord Jesus came to give the garment of praise for the spirit of heaviness, and He offers Himself to us as the never-failing Holy Spirit of praise. What can we do but cry unto Him: "Have mercy upon me, O Lord . . . that I may shew forth all thy praise"; and then take a deliberate stand in an act of faith and will: "I will bless the Lord at all times: his praise shall continually be in my mouth. . . . O magnify the Lord with me, and let us exalt His name together." Sometimes it is not until we make some such definite "sacrifice of praise" to God, some specific commitment to praise Him, that we are enabled to praise no matter in what situation He may place us. It was when the burnt offering began in Hezekiah's restored temple that the song of the Lord began also; and although such a commitment may have to be renewed again and again, always it will be followed by song. *(Jer. 17:14; Isa. 61:3; Pss. 9:13-14; 34:1,3; 2 Chron. 29:27)*

The offering of praise sometimes turned the tide of battle in Old Testament story. Jehoshaphat, king of Judah (which in Hebrew means "praised"), faced with the armies of three invading kings, fasted and prayed with his people, encouraged their faith in God, and then appointed singers to praise the Lord. They went before the army, praising God for His mercy; and when the people began to sing and to praise, God caused them to conquer the enemy. God's people gained a mighty victory, were given spoil in abundance, and returned to Jerusalem with joy: such is the power of praise. (2 Chron. 20)

Following the offering of praise, Solomon's newly opened temple was filled with God's holy presence. After the sacred ark had been brought into the temple, the trumpeters and singers began to praise the Lord, saying "For he is good; for his mercy endureth for ever." Then "the house was filled with a cloud ... so that the priests could not stand to minister by reason of the cloud: for the glory of the Lord had filled the house of God." And the offering of praise can bring an infilling of God's glory and presence today. (2 Chron. 5:13-14)

In seeking to praise when things are difficult, we must make much use of Scripture, even if only in a fragmentary manner. We must repeat continually the promises, the passages of praise, and the doxologies, laying them on our hearts and asking the Spirit to make them real in our experience until finally they do become our own in practical outworking.

Likewise, we must memorize the great hymns of the church and sing them to ourselves deliberately, alone if need be, and even through tears, until their mighty truths bear their holy fruit in our souls. We must surround ourselves with good recordings of fine sacred music and listen to them often. We must talk with our friends about the greatness and goodness of our God and praise Him together with them. We must raise our Ebenezer, our Stone of Help, and not only look at it frequently ourselves, but point others to its witness.

Such God-honoring faith we must not only seek, but must actively cultivate, even within the confines of our hedges—for "praise is the only answer."[35]

MY HEART IS RESTING

My heart is resting, O my God,
  I will give thanks and sing:
My heart is at the secret source
  Of every precious thing.
Now the frail vessel Thou hast made
  No hand but Thine shall fill:
For the waters of the earth have failed,
  And I am thirsty still.

I thirst for springs of heavenly life,
  And here all day they rise;
I seek the treasure of Thy love,
  And close at hand it lies.
And a new song is in my mouth,
  To long-loved music set:
"Glory to Thee for all the grace
  I have not tasted yet;

"Glory to Thee for strength withheld,
  For want and weakness known,
And the fear that sends me to Thy breast
  For what is most my own."
I have a heritage of joy
  That yet I cannot see:
But the hand that bled to make it mine
  Is keeping it for me.

My heart is resting, O my God,
  My heart is in Thy care;
I hear the voice of joy and health
  Resounding everywhere.
"Thou art my Portion, saith my soul,"
  Ten thousand voices say,
And the music of their glad Amen
  Will never die away. [11]

17

SLEEPLESSNESS

One of the greatest difficulties with which most sufferers have to contend is an inability to sleep. While the rest of the world welcomes the onset of night as happy respite from the burdens of the day and sinks effortlessly into deep and refreshing slumber, most sufferers watch the gathering shadows deepen with apprehension; for trying as the day may have been, the night brings heavier trials. Sleep is evasive, fitful, often impossible; energy ebbs; pain intensifies; fears seem more cogent, worries more pressing. We repeat to ourselves some of the promises concerning sleep: "When thou liest down, thou shalt not be afraid: yea, thou shalt lie down, and thy sleep shall be sweet"; "I will both lay me down in peace, and sleep: for thou, Lord, only makest me dwell in safety"; "he giveth his beloved sleep"—but such words almost mock us. Rather, ours seem to be the words of Job: "Wearisome nights are appointed to me.... I am full of tossings to and fro unto the dawning of the day." How shall we cope with a problem like this, particularly if, as is usually the case, it is a continuing problem? (Prov. 3:24; Pss. 4:8; 127:2; Job 7:3-4)

The writer of Psalm 77 had such a problem. "I cried unto

God with my voice, even unto God with my voice; and he gave ear unto me. In the day of my trouble I sought the Lord: my sore ran in the night, and ceased not: my soul refused to be comforted. I remembered God, and was troubled: I complained, and my spirit was overwhelmed. Thou holdest mine eyes waking: I am so troubled that I cannot speak. . . . Will the Lord cast off for ever? and will he be favourable no more? Is his mercy clean gone for ever? doth his promise fail for evermore? Hath God forgotten to be gracious? hath he in anger shut up his tender mercies?" (Ps. 77:1-4, 7-9)

But weary and discouraged as he was, the sleepless psalmist, probably by an act of sheer will power, determined to press beyond his afflictions on to the contemplation of his God. His outlook changed. He was able to analyze his difficulty and to see past it to its solution:

"And I said, This is my infirmity: but I will remember the years of the right hand of the most High. I will remember the works of the Lord: surely I will remember thy wonders of old. I will meditate also of all thy work, and talk of thy doings. Thy way, O God, is in the sanctuary: who is so great a God as our God? Thou art the God that doest wonders: thou hast declared thy strength among the people." (Ps. 77:10-14)

And throughout the remainder of Psalm 77, and through all of the next six psalms, the psalmist goes on to recount God's mercies and to sing His praise.

There is no doubt that those who must face continual sleeplessness or restless, fitful sleep have a very real problem, a true infirmity. Only those who have been confronted with it can know how inexpressibly wearing and devitalizing it is; how it saps away the very energy which is the physical basis of our ability to trust in God and to stay our hearts upon Him; how it seeks to erode the very roots of our faith. Yet God, who has said that He knows our downsittings and uprisings, who is acquainted with all our ways, has not left these sufferers without a way of escape. (Ps. 139:1-3)

"The day is thine, the night also is thine" wrote the psalmist. God is just as sovereign when we are wakeful as when sleep comes easily to our eyelids. "*Thou holdest mine eyes waking,*" he reminded himself. Our sleeplessness is not the result of some blind chance or capricious evil spirit. Therefore, our attitude towards it must be that of acceptance, even though chronic insomnia is a most difficult situation to have to accept. (*Pss. 74:16; 77:4*)

Actually, from a purely medical viewpoint, to resist sleeplessness is the surest way to allow it to gain the ascendancy over us; for as soon as we begin to worry about our wakefulness, we become more tense, and it grows increasingly difficult to relax and sleep. By accepting the situation as part of the hedge placed about us by our all-knowing, all-loving Father and trusting Him to uphold us whether we sleep or not, we are putting ourselves in the best possible position for sleep to overtake us.

Doctors tell us that although we may not be able to sleep, it is possible for us to rest; and this is something that every sleepless person must learn to do. What better way can there be than to rest in the Lord and wait patiently for Him? God will give rest of heart to those who seek it. "The Spirit of the Lord caused him to rest," wrote Isaiah. We are not alone in our weary vigils, for the One who keeps us neither slumbers nor sleeps. (*Ps. 37:7; Isa. 63:14*)

> He gives His angels charge o'er those who sleep,
> But He Himself watches with those who wake.[24]

The Lord Jesus died for us, that whether we wake or sleep, we should know His presence and share His life. (*1 Thess. 5:10*)

Even though our bodies may toss wearily to and fro, our hearts can learn to be still before the Lord. God will communicate His own stillness and strength to us in the night watches. It is our part to be still and to know deep within our hearts that He is God; so shall we see the salvation of the Lord. "Their strength is to sit still." (*Isa. 30:7*)

God has promised quietness to His people. "The work of righteousness shall be peace; and the effect of righteousness quietness and assurance for ever," He tells us. Quiet does not come easily to our turbulent human hearts, particularly if we are unable to sleep while others rest. But the God of all quiet watches with His children through the long vigils of the night, and "he giveth quietness." (*Isa. 32:17; Job 34:29*)

Many are the saints who have sought God in the long, still hours of the night and whose souls have been enriched with the treasures of darkness He has revealed to them. David found that he was enabled to keep God's law when he remembered His name in the night, and he steadfastly purposed to be faithful to Him, even in the night of trouble and sorrow. "Thou hast visited me in the night," he wrote, "thou hast tried me, and shalt find nothing; I am purposed that my mouth shall not transgress." We must entertain no complaint nor controversy with God concerning our sleeplessness if we would make grace to grow in this winter of our souls, but must stay our minds on God Himself and on His Word. If, like the blessed man of the first psalm, the law of the Lord is our delight and our meditation day and night, we, too, shall be like a tree planted by the rivers of water, bringing forth fruit with unwithered leaves. In God's law lies our strength to be faithful to Him, whether we meditate on it in the sunlight or in the darkness of pain-filled nights. We must constantly cry to God to keep us from sin in the night watches and pray that the meditation of our hearts may be acceptable to Him. (*Pss. 119:55; 17:3; 19:14*)

God is the giver of songs in the night; and how many songs have been given to saints who have had to seek the Lord through darkness and wakefulness! David's tears were his food day and night, yet he experienced God's loving-kindness in the daytime, and His songs were with him in the night. David found that soul-satisfaction and praise were his when he remembered God upon his bed and meditated on Him in the night watches. Many and rich are the songs we have in Christian literature from those who have been enabled to "sing aloud upon their beds." *(Job 35:10; Pss. 42:3, 8; 63:5-7; 149:5)*

But it is one thing to talk about songs in the night and another thing to realize them, as everyone who has had to live with a continuing insomnia knows. No matter how we seek to embrace our problem and to take from it all the good that God wishes to give us through it, there will be times when, like David, we will cry: "Have mercy upon me, O Lord; for I am weak: O Lord, heal me. . . . I am weary with my groaning . . . I water my couch with my tears." At such times we must remember that we are not alone even though we do not feel God's nearness, any more than we were when His realized presence enabled us to sing in the midst of our pain. *(Ps. 6:2, 6)*

Even if we have lost all sense of His closeness, our unsleeping, unchanging, sovereign, covenant-keeping God is watching with us and over us. He Himself passed through a night of darkness deeper than anything we can ever imagine, let alone be called upon to experience; and because for our sakes He was forsaken of the Father, we shall never be forsaken. His is the faithfulness in which we trust, His the strength by which we live, His the grace by which we can be strengthened to endure; and that unfailing source of supply depends not upon our poor, human frailty, nor our ability to feel His presence with us, but on the eternal God Himself.

We must rest upon Him, be still before Him, even claim something of His song, whether we have any consciousness of His nearness or not. Even when beset by the terror of night, we stake our all upon His promise and throw our whole weight, body and soul, upon our Savior; and we find Him faithful. "Weeping may endure for a night, but joy cometh in the morning." *(Ps. 30:5)*

SWEET SAVOR

Beloved, yield thy time to God, for He
  Will make eternity thy recompense;
Give all thy substance for His Love, and be
  Beatified past earth's experience.

Serve Him in bonds, until He set thee free;
  Serve Him in dust, until He lift thee thence;
Till death be swallowed up in victory
  When the great trumpet sounds to bid thee hence.

Shall setting day win day that will not set?
  Poor price wert thou to spend thyself for Christ,
Had not His wealth thy poverty sufficed:
  Yet since He makes His garden of thy clod,
Water thy lily, rose, or violet,
  And offer up thy sweetness unto God.[18]

18

AFFLICTIONS

"I know, O Lord, that thy judgments are right, and that thou in faithfulness hast afflicted me." (Ps. 119:75)

Afflictions of one kind or another come to most people at some time during their life, but for those who must live within one of God's hedges, affliction is likely to be a permanent thing, for it is some kind of affliction that constitutes the hedge. Such trials come to the Christian by no mere chance, but directly from the hand of the Father. The more clearly we can see and accept this, the easier it will be for us to learn to live in triumph within the confines of our own particular prison.

The saints of old took their afflictions from the hand of God. "The Almighty hath afflicted me," was Naomi's report to her people when she returned from Moab bereft of her husband and both her sons: "I went out full, and the Lord hath brought me home again empty." "The Lord hath afflicted me," lamented Jeremiah; "He hath . . . brought me into darkness, but not into light. . . . He hath hedged me about, that I cannot get out: he hath made my chain heavy." "He hath loosed my cord, and afflicted me," declared the tormented Job. (*Ruth* 1:20-21; *Lam.* 1:12; 3:2, 7; *Job 30:11*)

When sudden disaster strikes, it is natural to look at the variety of human elements that helped shape our trouble. We regret bitterly this or that which we might or might not have done, which could have contributed to or might have prevented the calamity; often we reproach ourselves and suffer deeply, unable to forgive ourselves for something that seems to have brought such grief into our own lives or lives of the ones we love. Human error may, indeed, enter into many of the trials that beset us and is always to be regretted; carelessness or rash judgments are never to be condoned. But for the committed Christian who is truly walking with God, such things can never be primary causes: all that comes to us comes from the hand of God and for His sovereign purpose.

Why God allows severe trials to enter the lives of His children, even to hedge them about, is one of the oldest questions in the universe; the problem of pain has engaged the finest and most devoted minds from time immemorial and has never yet been satisfactorily resolved. We believe that one day our God will make plain to His children the inscrutability of His ways; that in that golden morning when we shall know as we are known, every question will be forever stilled, and we shall be eternally satisfied with His explanation. Until then, we accept from His hand all that comes into our lives and seek to glorify Him in and through it. The entire human race is subject to suffering—"the same afflictions are accomplished in your brethren that are in the world"; but only the Christian has hope of final answers to life's mysteries. How much easier to take our sorrows from the Father's hand, knowing His presence with us now and having His promise of light ahead, than to suffer alone and in the dark! (1 *Pet.* 5:9)

"I have chosen thee in the furnace of affliction," God may tell some of His children; but He also says, "Fear not: for I have redeemed thee, I have called thee by thy name; thou art mine. When thou passest through the waters, I will be with

124

thee; and through the rivers, they shall not overflow thee: when thou walkest through the fire, thou shalt not be burned; neither shall the flame kindle upon thee. For I am the Lord thy God, the Holy One of Israel, thy Savior." (Isa. 48:10; 43:1-3)

God is not only with us in our afflictions, but He Himself shares them. God suffered with His ancient people Israel, and the angel of His presence saved them. He watches over us in our afflictions, setting and maintaining that boundary beyond which He will not permit the Evil One to pass; and it is His presence with us in our trials that saves us from their inherent evil. (Isa. 63:9)

When God has accomplished in us that purpose for which He has allowed our afflictions to come to us, He terminates them either here or in heaven. "Thus saith the Lord. . . . Though I have afflicted thee, I will afflict thee no more. . . I . . . will burst thy bonds in sunder." He told Nahum that although Israel's enemies should be folded together as thorns, in His own good time they should be devoured as dry stubble. What a promise for the afflicted soul! When God has finished with the hedge of thorn He has placed about us, He will consume it and set us free. (Nah. 1:12-13)

Meantime, He succors us as we live with our problems. He hears the cry of His afflicted ones and will have mercy upon them. He has promised to be our strength, our fortress, and our refuge in the day of affliction. His Word is our comfort, no matter how great the trial. (Job 34:28; Jer. 16:19)

God has promised to deliver us, not necessarily from our afflictions themselves, but from the evil that Satan would work through them. Sometimes He delivers us *out of* our many afflictions, and sometimes *in* them; but always He delivers us *from evil.* (Ps. 34:19; Job 36:15)

He has also promised that He will bring glory to Himself out of our afflictions and that we shall receive spiritual blessings through them. It was in the land of affliction that God caused Joseph to be fruitful, by him preserving Israel through whom He was later to give to the world both His written and

His Living Word. He so enriched the soul of the psalmist that he was able to declare: "It is good for me that I have been afflicted; that I might learn thy statutes. Before I was afflicted I went astray: but now have I kept thy word." (Gen. 41:52; Ps. 119:71, 67)

Paul taught new believers not to be surprised if they suffered afflictions, but to expect them. When sending Timothy to comfort and establish the Thessalonian Christians who had suffered much, he urged that they should not be moved by afflictions, for all Christians must expect them. He warned that they would suffer tribulation for Christ's sake and said that the news of their triumph over their troubles comforted Paul in his own trials. (1 Thess. 1:6; 3:1-7)

Paul urged Timothy to be a partaker of the afflictions of the Gospel, according to the power of God, and exhorted him to endure afflictions. He wrote his Corinthian letters out of much affliction and anguish of heart, with many tears, and taught believers that our trials are meant to work us heavenly good, that our light affliction is working nothing less than glory for us if we look not at things visible and temporal, but at things unseen and eternal. (2 Tim. 1:8; 4:5; 2 Cor. 2:4; 4:17-18)

Writing to the Colossian Christians, Paul spoke even more significantly about his afflictions, pointing out that through our sufferings we may come to share in the sufferings of the Savior Himself, even suffering vicariously for the spiritual good of others. "I . . . now rejoice in my sufferings for you," he wrote, "and fill up that which is behind of the afflictions of Christ in my flesh for his body's sake, which is the church: whereof I am made a minister, according to the dispensation of God which is given to me for you, to fulfill the word of God." Whatever these verses may actually mean in practical experience, it is quite clear that God has a purpose in the afflictions He sends to His children, that that purpose is both high and holy, and that we are called to share in that purpose. (Col. 1:23-25)

That we might know God and live in His presence forever,

our Savior was afflicted in measure greater than anything we can ever experience. Despised and rejected by men, a man of sorrows and acquainted with grief, oppressed and afflicted, He bore our griefs and carried our sorrows: shall He not succor us and meet our every need? Read the entire, moving 53rd chapter of Isaiah and compare your own "light affliction" to that of the Holy One when you need strength to carry on!

For it is this Savior who speaks to His afflicted children: "O thou afflicted, tossed with tempest, and not comforted, behold, I will lay thy stones with fair colours, and lay thy foundations with sapphires. And I will make thy windows of agates, and thy gates of carbuncles, and all thy borders of pleasant stones. And all thy children shall be taught of the Lord; and great shall be the peace of thy children. . . . This is the heritage of the servants of the Lord." (Isa. 54:11-13, 17)

If you are one of God's suffering ones, wandering this weary world destitute, afflicted, and tormented, God speaks these words particularly to you, living within the hedge of His choosing. May you be faithful to His high and holy calling. (Heb. 11:37)

A BETTER RESURRECTION

I have no wit, no words, no tears;
  My heart within me, like a stone,
Is numbed too much for hopes or fears;
  Look right, look left, I dwell alone.
I lift mine eyes, but dimmed with grief
  No everlasting hills I see:
My life is in the falling leaf—
      O Jesus, quicken me!

My life is like a faded leaf;
  My harvest dwindled to a husk;
Truly my life is void and brief
  And tedious in the barren dusk;
My life is like a frozen thing;
  No bud nor greenness can I see;
Yet rise it shall, the sap of Spring—
      O Jesus, rise in me!

My life is like a broken bowl,
  A broken bowl that cannot hold
One drop of water for my soul,
  Or cordial in the searching cold.
Cast in the fire the perished thing;
  Melt and remould it, till it be
A royal cup for Him, my King—
      O Jesus, drink of me![18]

19

OUT OF THE DEPTHS

"Out of the depths have I cried unto thee, O Lord."

(Ps. 130:1)

Many times have God's people cried to Him out of the depths of troubles so profound that they despaired of ever being delivered from them, despaired even of life itself, and could only cry to God for help: "Save me, O God . . . I sink in deep mire, where there is no standing; I am come into deep waters, where the floods overflow me." And we, too, sometimes feel that the difficulties of our hedged-in lives are so great that they almost submerge us, as deep waters; then we, too, cry out: "Thou hast laid me in the lowest pit, in darkness, in the deeps." "Let not the waterflood overflow me, neither let the deep swallow me up." (Pss. 69:1-2; 88:6; 69:15)

The Scriptures relate how more than one of God's true servants became so discouraged that they actually longed for death to release them. Elijah was so intimidated by the threats of Jezebel that even after God had vindicated His name on Mount Carmel, the prophet begged that he might die, saying, "It is enough; now, O Lord, take away my life." Job cursed the

129

day of his birth and cried: "Why is light given to a man whose way is hid, and whom God hath hedged in?" And Jonah, even after his deliverance from the depths of the fish's belly, and after having seen Nineveh turn to God as a result of his preaching, prayed: "O Lord, take . . . my life from me; for it is better for me to die than to live." David, the man after God's own heart, wished for death more than once, exclaiming: "Oh that I had wings like a dove! for then would I fly away, and be at rest." (1 *Kings* 19:4; *Job* 3:23; *Jon.* 4:3; *Ps.* 55:6)

And sometimes we, too, feel that life within our particular hedge has become so intolerable that we long for death. It may be that we have borne troubles patiently for years and have seen and acknowledged God's hand in our trials; yet there can come a day when we think we can bear no more and we cry: "It is enough; now take away my life," for such is the weakness of our frail humanity.

When such depths threaten to overwhelm us, we can only stay our souls upon the sovereignty of God. It is by His design that we are experiencing these depths, and we are in His care. His love and grace are deeper than our woes, and He is in control of our circumstances. There are no depths which are beyond His knowledge and His power, no deep places where He cannot work out His holy purpose. "In his hand are the deep places of the earth. . . . The sea is his, and he made it." "Whatsoever the Lord pleased, that did he in heaven, and in earth, in the seas, and all deep places." (*Pss.* 95:4-5; 135:6)

The Scriptures give us many songs sung by those whom God had delivered out of the depths of trouble and sorrow. From them we can learn much about the attitudes of heart and mind that made it possible for God to effect their deliverance—and ours.

"I love the Lord, because he hath heard my voice and my supplication," exulted David. "The sorrows of death compassed me, and the pains of hell gat hold upon me: I found trouble and sorrow. Then called I upon the name of the Lord; O Lord, I beseech thee, deliver my soul. Gracious is the

Lord, and righteous; yea, our God is merciful. . . . I was brought low, and he helped me. . . . Thou hast delivered my soul from death, mine eyes from tears, and my feet from falling." (Ps. 116:1, 3-6, 8)

Probably no one in history has sounded the depths quite so literally as poor Jonah in the belly of the great fish; yet even there he cried to God, and God delivered him. "I cried by reason of mine affliction unto the Lord, and he heard me; out of the belly of hell cried I, and thou heardest my voice. For thou hadst cast me into the deep, in the midst of the seas; and the floods compassed me about: all thy billows and thy waves passed over me. . . . The waters compassed me about . . . the weeds were wrapped about my head. . . . When my soul fainted within me I remembered the Lord: and my prayer came in unto thee, into thine holy temple. . . . I will sacrifice unto thee with the voice of thanksgiving; I will pay that that I have vowed. Salvation is of the Lord." (Jon. 2:2-3, 5, 7, 9)

Jonah's sufferings were his own fault, for he had run away from God, refusing to obey His commands; yet even so, God heard his cry. What comfort this should bring to the many who suffer as Job did: their sufferings caused not by deliberate sin, but allowed by God for His own inscrutable purpose! In his song of deliverance Jonah tells how he came before the Lord in his trouble. *He thought upon God's law:* "I will look again toward the holy temple"; *he contemplated the character and attributes of God:* "I remembered the Lord"; *he worshiped God in confession and intent of obedience:* "I will sacrifice unto thee with the voice of thanksgiving; I will pay that that I have vowed"; *he acknowledged God's sovereignty:* "Salvation is of the Lord." So we, too, may come to God and seek His deliverance; and seeking Him in this divinely appointed manner, we know that we shall not seek Him in vain. (Jon. 2:4, 7, 9)

The sorely afflicted writer of Psalm 102 graphically describes the depths of his woes in the first eleven verses and then moves on to the contemplation of his sovereign God: "But thou, O Lord, shalt endure for ever; and thy remembrance unto all generations. ... Of old hast thou laid the foundation of the earth: and the heavens are the work of thy hands. They shall perish, but thou shalt endure: yea, all of them shall wax old like a garment; as a vesture shalt thou change them, and they shall be changed: but thou art the same, and thy years shall have no end. ... This shall be written for the generation to come: and the people which shall be created shall praise the Lord." It is with this unchanging and unchangeable God that we have to do. "This God is our God for ever and ever: he will be our guide even unto death." And God will yet make the deep and dark places of our experience too, to sound forth His praise. (Pss. 102:12, 25-27, 18; 48:14)

Need His children then be overwhelmed by the depths through which He asks them to go? "He divided the sea, and caused them to *pass through*; and he made the waters to stand as an heap"; it is His purpose to bring us through the waters, not to have us be lost in their depths. He has promised that He will go through their depths with us: "When thou passest through the waters, I will be with thee; and through the rivers, they shall not overflow thee"; "for I the Lord thy God will hold thy right hand, saying unto thee, Fear not; I will help thee." And someday, in His own good time, we shall hear Him say to us, finally and forever, "I will dry up thy rivers." (Ps. 78:13; Isa. 43:2; 41:13; 44:27)

Shall we fear to trust Him who for our sakes passed through the dark waters of death itself? Deeper than even those grim depths is His love, passing knowledge in all its breadth, length, depth, and height. And "who shall separate us from the love of Christ? shall tribulation, or distress, or persecution, or famine, or nakedness, or peril, or sword? ... Nay, in all these things we are more than conquerors through him that loved us. For I am persuaded, that neither death, nor life, nor angels, nor principalities, nor powers, nor things present, nor things to come, nor height, nor *depth*, nor any other creature, shall be able to separate us from the love of God, which is in Christ Jesus our Lord." *(Eph. 3:18-19; Rom. 8:35, 37-39)*

AGAINST THAT DAY

"For I know whom I have believed, and am persuaded that he is able to keep that which I have committed unto him against that day." (2 Tim. 1:12)

Against what day?
    The day of great temptation
      When powers of ill,
    Subtle and strong, would overwhelm the fortress
      Of mind and will.

Against what day?
    The day when sudden anguish
      Crushes the soul;
    When ruthless pain and cold, relentless sorrow
      Take bitter toll.

Against what day?
    The day of swift destruction,
      When in a day
    The slowly-garnered treasures of a lifetime
      Are swept away.

Against what day?
    The day when Death's grey angel
      Crosses my door,
    Blotting out life's sweet song and golden sunshine
      Forevermore.

Against that day,
    That day of dread,
When strong heart faileth
    And hope is fled,

Day of life's direst need
    Or Death's dark sleep,
I am persuaded that my God is able
    My soul to keep![1]

20

THE EVIL DAY

For the most part, our thinking has been directed towards those who must endure longstanding sorrow or pain, those who for months, years, even a lifetime, have had to live within the restrictions of one of God's hedges, and some of whom must live there in the knowledge that no escape is possible this side of heaven.

There is, however, another kind of evil to which mortal man is subject and from which Christians are not excluded: the evil of sudden, unexpected, catastrophic calamity. Swift and horrible death, striking down loved ones in the prime of life or in childhood; sudden mental collapse in one of brilliant and dedicated mind; suicide in the family circle; the bizarre type of accident wherein a fine violinist may suffer a slight mishap and come to no great bodily harm except to sustain a permanent injury to one finger, and that the index finger on his left hand; the incredible horror experienced by one whose entire family is wiped out by fire, flood, or accident—what has the Word of God to say to help us in such an evil hour?

This is the kind of catastrophe of which we read in the book of Job. Perfect, upright, a man who feared God and shunned evil, offering sacrifices not only on his own behalf, but also for his sons and daughters lest any of them should have forgotten God in some way, the prosperous head of a great and wealthy household: Job flourished. But then "there was a day," and in that day unspeakable destruction descended upon Job, his family, and all that he had. *(Job 1:6, 13)*

Such evils are all too familiar in human history; every morning's newspaper is saturated with them. And there are few people whose personal history, in one way or another, is not marked by some such day, after which life can never again be the same.

Such "days" are the work of Satan: "an enemy hath done this." But the Enemy works within God's sovereignty and is not permitted to exceed His bounds. God has His own reasons for allowing such attacks. He has not promised to explain His ways to us here, although the trusting soul is likely to be given glimmerings of His design and is certain to be given assurances as to the ultimate end of such testings. We believe that the day will come when He will make all things plain, and we shall be able to say, like Joseph, "As for you, ye thought evil against me; but God meant it unto good . . . as it is this day"; or with Israel, "Our God turned the curse into a blessing." Meanwhile, we trust Him and seek to fortify our souls against spiritual loss in the evil hour. *(Matt. 13:28; Gen. 50:20; Neh. 13:2)*

For God has promised that we shall triumph in the evil hour and has made provision by means of which we may do so. It is up to us to seek out these provisions and to learn to use them; for when sudden evil strikes, the soul who has not already learned to use God's armor will have no opportunity to learn to do so then. We are urged to remember our Creator early, before the evil days come, and he is a wise Christian who does so. *(Eccles. 12:1)*

Our greatest bulwark against sudden calamity is our knowledge of Jesus Christ and our standing in Him: "For I know whom I have believed, and am persuaded that he is able to keep that which I have committed unto him against that day."

Those whose trust is in Him may suffer evil, but they shall not be overwhelmed by it; "They shall not be ashamed in the evil time." (2 Tim. 1:2; Ps. 37:19)

God has provided a holy armor to defend His children against the Enemy's attacks, and we are told to "put on the whole armour of God, that [we] may be able to stand against the wiles of the devil. For we wrestle not against flesh and blood, but against principalities, against powers, against the rulers of the darkness of this world, against spiritual wickedness in high places.

"Wherefore take unto you the whole armour of God, that ye may be able to withstand in the evil day, and having done all, to stand. Stand therefore, having your loins girt about with truth, and having on the breastplate of righteousness; and your feet shod with the preparation of the gospel of peace; above all, taking the shield of faith, wherewith ye shall be able to quench all the fiery darts of the wicked. And take the helmet of salvation, and the sword of the Spirit, which is the word of God: praying always with all prayer and supplication in the Spirit." He who is wearing that armor is unlikely to be overcome, in the evil hour. (Eph. 6:11-18)

God says that we shall be able to "withstand in the evil day, and having done all, to stand." There are times when we may be able to "withstand" Satan and possibly drive the powers of darkness back and win new ground for the Kingdom of God; there may be other times when all we will be able to do is to "stand"—to suffer no spiritual loss in the evil hour. But God is able to make us stand; this is our confidence as we contemplate the evil day. (Eph. 6:13; Rom. 14:4)

God has told us that we need not fear such an hour of testing. "*Thou shalt not be afraid* for the terror by night; nor for the arrow that flieth by day; nor for the pestilence that walketh in darkness; nor for the destruction that wasteth at noonday"; "*neither shalt thou be afraid* of destruction when it cometh." "*He shall not be afraid* of evil tidings: his heart is fixed, trusting in the Lord." "Yea, though I walk through the valley of the shadow of death, *I will fear no evil;* for thou art with me; thy rod and thy staff they comfort me." Sudden evil may come to us, as to all in the human family; but we need not live in its fear all our days, nor fear that it will rob us of our spiritual treasure if it comes. *(Ps. 91:5-6; Job 5:21; Pss. 112:7; 23:4)*

The way we live from day to day when things are going smoothly will determine in large measure whether we shall stand or fall in the evil hour. When we walk humbly and patiently in God's strength on the plains, then we may expect Him to keep us from the perils of the mountains or the valleys.

The Great Intercessor is not unmindful of the evil hour as He prays for His own before the throne of God. "Satan hath desired to have you, that he may sift you as wheat," He told the impetuous Peter, "but I have prayed for thee, that thy faith fail not." And Peter's faith did not fail: Peter failed, but his faith stood the test, and Peter became one of the pillars of the early Christian church. "I pray not that thou shouldest take them out of the world, but that thou shouldest keep them from the evil," prayed the Savior, and that is still His prayer for His children. And in the strength of that prayer His obedient children have every right to trust. *(Luke 22:31-32; John 17:15)*

We read that when Job's ten children and all that he had were swept away in the devastation of his evil hour: "Then Job arose, and rent his mantle, and shaved his head, and fell down upon the ground, *and worshipped,* and said, Naked came I out of my mother's womb, and naked shall I return thither: the Lord gave, and the Lord hath taken away; blessed be the name of the Lord." When Abraham was commanded by God to sacrifice Isaac, as he drew near to Mount Moriah where he was to carry out this excruciating task, he said to his servants: "Abide ye here . . . I and the lad will go yonder *and worship.*" When the Lord Jesus contemplated His approaching evil hour, more fraught with evil than any hour in history, He prayed, saying: "Now is my soul troubled; and what shall I say? Father, save me from this hour: but for this cause came I unto this hour. Father, *glorify thy name.*" (*Job 1:20-21; Gen. 22:5; John 12:27-28*)

And so we must face the evil hour. Like the human Savior, we shrink from it. But we have been told not to fear it; we have been provided with the armor necessary for triumph; we have the assurances of God's promises, the Savior's prayers, and the Spirit's enabling for the battle. Our part is to worship, whatever God may send us, and to pray—not so much for deliverance as that God may glorify His name through us. Such God-honoring faith in the evil hour proclaims to the whole hierarchy of hell the power and reality of the life of God in the soul of man; and it shall not go unrewarded.

If God calls us so to glorify Him, may we be found faithful!

PERFECT PEACE

Like a river glorious
   Is God's perfect peace,
Over all victorious
   In its bright increase;
Perfect, yet it floweth
   Fuller every day;
Perfect, yet it groweth
   Deeper all the way.

Hidden in the hollow
   Of His blessed hand,
Never foe can follow,
   Never traitor stand;
Not a surge of worry,
   Not a shade of care,
Not a blast of hurry
   Touch the spirit there.

Every joy or trial
   Falleth from above,
Traced upon our dial
   By the Sun of Love.
We may trust Him fully
   All for us to do;
They who trust Him wholly
   Find Him wholly true.

        Stayed upon Jehovah,
           Hearts are fully blest,
        Finding, as He promised,
           Perfect peace and rest.[37]

21

WHEN ...

The evil day descends upon mankind swiftly and suddenly, giving no warning. One moment skies are clear and smiling; the next, sunlight may be blotted out, possibly forever.

Other than to walk closely with the Savior from day to day and to learn to put on and use the whole armor of God, there is nothing we can do to prepare our souls for sudden catastrophe. Certainly we cannot prevent it. But the mighty promises of God may be used "in sunshine weather"[9] to fortify our hearts against such eventualities. The soul that has taken care to hedge itself about with the Word of God need have no fear of the evil day.

God has a multiplicity of specific "when's" for His troubled children, and a study of such promises can help arm us for the conflicts of life. He has told us when we are to think upon His word and His commandments: "*when* thou sittest in thine house, and *when* thou walkest by the way, and *when* thou liest down, and *when* thou risest up." The soul so steeped in God is unlikely to be shaken in the evil day. (*Deut. 6:7*)

There are "when's" for particular evils and occasions as well.

There is no cloud without His presence, and the certainty of His remembered covenant: "When I bring a cloud over the earth ... the bow shall be seen in the cloud; and I will remember my covenant." We are sure of our Savior's guidance and presence with us wherever He may lead us: "When he putteth forth his own sheep, he goeth before them." He will bring us through all evils unharmed in spirit: "When thou passest through the waters, I will be with thee; and through the rivers, they shalt not overflow thee: when thou walkest through the fire, thou shalt not be burned; neither shall the flame kindle upon thee." He has promised us freedom from fear: "When thou liest down, thou shalt not be afraid." (Gen. 9:14-15; John 10:4; Isa. 43:2; Prov. 3:24)

He has covenanted to supply our human needs: "When the poor and needy seek water, and there is none, and their tongue faileth for thirst, I the Lord will hear them, I the God of Israel will not forsake them. I will open rivers in high places, and fountains in the midst of the valleys: I will make the wilderness a pool of water, and the dry land springs of water." When every resource fails, still we have God: "When my father and my mother forsake me, then the Lord will take me up." God is sovereign and in control of all the forces of His universe: "When the waves thereof arise, thou stillest them." God will perfect that which concerns us. (Isa. 41:17-18; Pss. 27:10; 89:9; 138:8)

But how weak is the human heart, how loath to trust in its God! We, too, have our "when's" as we contemplate the evil hour. "When I looked for good, then evil came unto me: and when I waited for light, there came darkness," we cry. "When shall I arise, and the night be gone?" we ask; "when shall I come and appear before God?" Thus we are tempted to feel when trouble comes upon us; we long to evade it or escape it. (Job 30:26; 7:4; Ps. 42:2)

Yet the Scriptures are rich with the witness of those who have found God true in the midst of trouble and who have triumphed through His faithfulness. Listen to their testimony:

"When the wicked, even mine enemies and my foes, came upon me to eat up my flesh, they stumbled and fell"; "when a man's ways please the Lord, he maketh even his enemies to be at peace with him." "When my spirit was overwhelmed within me, then thou knewest my path." "When I fall, I shall arise; when I sit in darkness, the Lord shall be a light unto me"; "what time (when) I am afraid, I will trust in thee." "From the end of the earth will I cry unto thee, when my heart is overwhelmed: lead me to the rock that is higher than I." "My soul shall be satisfied as with marrow and fatness; and my mouth shall praise thee with joyful lips: when I remember thee upon my bed, and meditate on thee in the night watches"; "when I awake, I am still with thee." (Ps. 27:2; Prov. 16:7; Ps. 142:3; Mic. 7:8; Pss. 56:3; 61:2; 63:5-6; 139:18)

Obedience is the key to such fellowship with God, as David knew well: "When thou saidst, Seek ye my face; my heart said unto thee, Thy face, Lord, will I seek." We, too, must set ourselves to seek His face and the strength of His promises, if we would know triumph in the evil day. (Ps. 27:8)

Paul had a thorn in the flesh, for whose removal he besought the Lord three times, only to have his request denied, but Paul went on from strength to strength. "He said unto me, My grace is sufficient for thee: for my strength is made perfect in weakness. Most gladly therefore will I rather glory in my infirmities, that the power of Christ may rest upon me. Therefore I take pleasure in infirmities, in reproaches, in necessities, in persecutions, in distresses for Christ's sake: for when I am weak, then am I strong." And God still allows weakness to remain with His children, that His strength may be realized and His people may learn this profound truth. (2 Cor. 12:9-10)

When King Hezekiah restored the temple worship in Jerusalem, he prepared the sacrifices and commanded that they be offered; and we read that "when the burnt offering began, the song of the Lord began also. . . . and all the congregation worshipped." And so it is with us. When we are willing to let

God work out His holy will in us, even if it must be by pain and weakness, we will find His joy in our hearts and His song upon our lips. (2 Chron. 29:27-28)

And well may we rejoice. Not for one minute will God forget His own; glorious is the destiny He has in store for those who love Him. "They that feared the Lord spake often one to another: and the Lord hearkened, and heard it, and a book of remembrance was written before him for them that feared the Lord, and that thought upon his name. And they shall be mine, saith the Lord of hosts, in that day when I make up my jewels." What a hope is ours! "Beloved, now are we the sons of God, and it doth not yet appear what we shall be: but we know that, when he shall appear, we shall be like him; for we shall see him as he is." No weakness then—no pain, no sorrow; we shall be like our Savior. And in that shining hour, life's mysteries will be explained, and we shall learn the "why" of the thorns that have hedged us in so sharply while on earth. "His servants shall serve him: and they shall see his face; and his name shall be in their foreheads." Can any trial be too great whose ultimate end is such glory? (Mal. 3:16-17; 1 John 3:2; Rev. 22:3-4)

Wherefore, "now, little children, abide in him; that when he shall appear, we may have confidence, and not be ashamed before him at his coming." (1 John 2:28)

THROUGH FAITH

Through faith we understand
   The things we cannot know—
The hidden pattern God has planned,
   And why each thread is so;
We trace life's vast design
   And lose His golden strand;
But when our wills with His entwine,
   Through faith we understand.

Through faith we understand
   What to our sight is dim,
And still Love's sweet, all-knowing hand
   Leads those who trust in Him.
Ours not to know the way,
   But bow to His command;
And when our childlike hearts obey,
   Through faith we understand.[1]

22

AND OTHERS . . .[32]

The eleventh chapter of the Book of Hebrews, that triumphant roll call of the heroes of faith, is familiar and dear to the hearts of all believers. Here faith is seen as a way of life that is pleasing to God. The chapter deals essentially with two types of things: things "hoped for" in the future, or rewards beyond this life, and things "not seen," or unseen divine realities. Without such an awareness of unseen divine realities and an assurance of future divine fulfillments, it is impossible to please God. Such faith is a primary condition of knowledge and is essential to the understanding of the origin of the universe; it is the foundation of all right thinking about those "worlds" which form the stage and setting of human history.[38]

The writer goes on to review the amazing accomplishments that such faith wrought in the lives of Old Testament saints. Sixteen well-known persons are named in verses 4 to 35, and a final unknown number are grouped together under the appellation of "the prophets." Great miracles took place in the lives of these heroes because of their God-honoring and God-pleasing faith, which God accounted to them as righteousness; and

147

it is thrilling to read this resumé of the widely varying revelations of God's power on behalf of His suffering but faithful and believing people. Yet none of these stalwarts actually reached the goal towards which their whole lives were directed, but pressed on in the assurance of its "hoped for" possession in that future with God in which the unseen divine realities, for which they had lived and died, would be realized. For God in His inscrutable sovereignty has decreed that not until the "better thing," which is to be the reward of those who believe in Christ, shall be given, will the Old Testament saints be crowned with the complete fulfillment of their heroic faith.

A significant change in this chapter takes place in the middle of verse 35. Until then, God had set His seal upon the faith and faithfulness of His believers here named by intervening in miracle on their behalf, so that through faith they "subdued kingdoms, wrought righteousness, obtained promises, stopped the mouths of lions, quenched the violence of fire, escaped the edge of the sword, out of weakness were made strong, waxed valiant in fight, turned to flight the armies of the aliens. Woman received their dead raised to life"—and then the change occurs, initiated by two small words, *and others*. "And *others* were tortured, not accepting deliverance; that they might obtain a better resurrection: *and others* had trial of cruel mockings and scourgings, yea, moreover of bonds and imprisonment: they were stoned, they were sawn asunder, were tempted, were slain with the sword: they wandered about in sheepskins and goatskins; being destitute, afflicted, tormented; (of whom the world was not worthy:) they wandered in deserts, and in mountains, and in dens and caves of the earth." (*Heb.* 11:33-38)

These unnamed saints, probably in number far exceeding the sixteen whose names are given us, experienced no miracle of deliverance in their evil hour, but were permitted to suffer horribly, often unto death. Was their faith, then, less than that of those whom God delivered? We are not told so. On the contrary, many of them were given opportunity to escape their tortures by denying their faith, but refused to accept such deliverance, thus sealing their commitment with their life's blood rather than be unfaithful to their God. Obviously there was nothing lacking in the quality of their faith.

And so as we contemplate this chapter, we are driven onto the horns of the dilemma of the ages. Here are two groups of people, some named, some unnamed: all lived by faith, pleasing God; all looked for the things "hoped for" and trusted in the divine reality of the things "not seen"; none grasped the whole of the promised reward until the fullness of God's time; a few knew miracle and deliverance in their lives, while many suffered unto death itself, without God's seeming intervention on their behalf.

What shall we say before the unfathomable mystery of the inscrutability of the sovereignty of our God? What but bow before Him in worship and in awe and exclaim with David: "I was dumb, I opened not my mouth; because thou didst it." (Ps. 39:9)

Paul considers this mystery in that part of his epistle to the Romans (chapters 9-12) where he discusses the relative positions of Israel and the Gentile nations, after the Savior's redeeming work had brought the Gentile believers into the covenant blessings previously reserved for Israel alone. He goes through three chapters of close reasoning, examining the evidence from every possible angle, and finally concludes: "O the depth of the riches both of the wisdom and knowledge of God! how unsearchable are his judgments, and his ways past finding out! For who hath known the mind of the Lord? or who hath been his counsellor? Or who hath first given to him, and it shall be recompensed unto him again? For of him, and through him, and to him, are all things: to whom be glory for ever. Amen." (Rom. 11:33-36)

From his examination of this inexplicable mystery of God's choice, Paul moves directly into a sublime exhortation which must be the faithful Christian's only response: "I beseech you therefore, brethren, by the mercies of God, that ye present your bodies a living sacrifice, holy, acceptable unto God, which is your reasonable service. And be not conformed to this world: but be ye transformed by the renewing of your mind, that ye may prove what is that good, and acceptable, and perfect, will of God." We can never hope to understand the mysteries of God with our finite minds, but there are two things we can and must do—present our bodies to God for the outworking of His purpose, whatever it may be; and prove in our own lives the goodness, the acceptability, and the perfection of the holy will of God. God's will cannot be understood, but it can be proved; and not in spite of, but because of God's inscrutability that is what we are challenged to do. (Rom. 12:1-2)

Similarly, the writer to the Hebrews moves immediately from his contemplation of the faithful saints and martyrs of the past to an exhortation to those who are still in the arena of battle. "Wherefore seeing we also are compassed about with so great a cloud of witnesses, let us lay aside every weight, and the sin which doth so easily beset us, and let us run with patience the race that is set before us, looking unto Jesus the author and finisher of our faith; who for the joy that was set before him endured the cross, despising the shame, and is set down at the right hand of the throne of God." (Heb. 12:2)

And these are God's commands to us today. We are His children, seeking to live lives of faith that will be pleasing to Him. We may be among those to whose faithful testimony His seal of miraculous deliverance has been given; or we may be among that throng, numberless and nameless, who are called upon to be faithful through a lifetime of undeserved, unexplained, and unrelieved suffering. What can we do but silently bow and worship, seeking His grace that we may be given the strength to "endure, as seeing him who is invisible"? We present our bodies to Him to be, literally if necessary, a living sacrifice; we prove His perfect will; we run with patience the race that is set before us, looking to our exalted Savior to keep us faithful to the end. (Heb. 11:27)

No one chooses to be the corn of wheat that falls into the earth to die, but the history of God's working in His saints, both in the pages of Scripture and out of them, shows that many are thus chosen by their Master to carry out their part in the eternal plan of God. If such be His choice for us, may we be faithful until we receive from our Lord Himself the crown of life.

IN HEAVENLY LOVE ABIDING

In heavenly love abiding,
  No change my heart shall fear:
And safe is such confiding,
  For nothing changes here:
The storm may roar without me,
  My heart may low be laid,
But God is round about me,
  And can I be dismayed?

Wherever He may guide me
  No want shall turn me back;
My Shepherd is beside me,
  And nothing can I lack.
His wisdom ever waketh,
  His sight is never dim;
He knows the way He taketh,
  And I will walk with Him.

Green pastures are before me,
  Which yet I have not seen:
Bright skies will soon be o'er me
  Where the dark clouds have been;
My hope I cannot measure,
  My path to life is free:
My Saviour has my treasure,
  And He will walk with me.[11]

23

DWELLING PLACE

We who must live within one of God's hedges must not consider this to be our only place of abode. God may not permit us to leave our fenced-in place of His choosing, but He does not confine us to its boundaries. For us, as for all His children, God has offered Himself as a dwelling place; and because of our special need of succor, who can say that we may not find in this aspect of our faithful God an especially real and rich blessing?

"Lord, thou hast been our dwelling place in all generations. Before the mountains were brought forth, or ever thou hadst formed the earth and the world, even from everlasting to everlasting, thou art God," declared Moses, the man of God. This God, so aptly described as our Eternal Home,[30] is even more: He is our Home even now, our strong Habitation, our Rock and Fortress in whom we may dwell in freedom and in joy even while we live from day to day within our hedges. Strong, indeed, is the dwelling place of those who have made the Lord their habitation, who have chosen to dwell in the rock, and there to dwell deep. (Pss. 90:1; 71:3; Num. 24:21; Ps. 91:9; Jer. 48:28; 49:8)

God has also promised to be a sanctuary to His children. Speaking of His chastened and dispersed people of the covenant, He gave His word through the prophet Ezekiel: "Thus saith the Lord God; Although I have cast them far off among the heathen, and although I have scattered them among the countries, yet will I be to them as a little sanctuary in the countries where they shall come." The sanctuary, besides speaking to Israel of God's presence in their midst and of forgiveness, acceptance, and worship, spoke to them of refuge; and all this God promised to be to His people, even while He allowed them to suffer His punishment for profaning His temple and neglecting His law. And all this He will be to us. "In the fear of the Lord is strong confidence: and his children shall have a place of refuge." "The eternal God is thy refuge, and underneath are the everlasting arms: and he shall thrust out the enemy from before thee." (Ezek. 11:16; Prov. 14:26; Deut. 33:27)

Those who have made God their sanctuary may be free from fear, for He alone is to be feared, and He gives Himself as a hiding place from all other fears. When we know God as our sanctuary, we begin to learn His ways and come to understand something of the hidden ways in which He has made us walk, for it was when the psalmist went into the sanctuary that he was able to understand both God's ways and his own painful circumstances. In the sanctuary we find strength and beauty, and there we learn to praise, to worship, and to serve our God. Many and rich are the blessings that God has promised to those who seek to know Him as their dwelling place, their habitation, and their sanctuary. (Isa. 8:12-13; Pss. 77:13; 73:16-17; 96:6; 150:1; 2 Chron. 30:8; Isa. 32:18; 33: 16, 24)

As if it were not enough that God should make Himself available to His children in such magnificent capacity, He has promised in infinite condescension that He, the God of heaven and earth, will make His dwelling place, His habitation, even His sanctuary in us. We read that He had compassion on His people and on His dwelling place; that He desired and chose Zion for His habitation; and that the heathen should acknowledge that He was the Lord when they would see Him sanctified in his people. "I chose no city . . . that my name might be therein; but I chose David," we read in 1 Kings 8:16; and so He chooses us today. (2 Chron. 36:15; Ps. 132:13-14; Lev. 10:3; Ezek. 20:41; 36:23)

And this He does in the full strength of the triune Godhead, for we read that the believer is indwelt by the Father, the Son, and the Holy Spirit. What unsearchable riches of glory are ours, to be thus united to the eternal God in such indissoluble bonds of intimacy and security: we in Him and He in us! Truly, God has made us to be complete in Himself, even though He may have hedged us in. (2 Cor. 6:16; Col. 1:27; 1 Cor. 3:16)

All God's promises are for all His people, of course; but human as we are, most of us only appropriate those of which we stand in desperate need. Those who know strong apparent security on earth may never come to realize God as their dwelling place; but those who must inhabit a thorny hedge in this life are ready enough to do so. The fear, the insecurity, and the pain that surround us are messengers of God to drive us to Himself, to help us find our life on earth, surrounded as it is by thorn, deep within the heart and life of the eternal Father Himself. May we stop short of nothing but the abundant supply for our deepest need that our sovereign Lord longs for us to experience.

And one day we, too, shall hear the great voice out of heaven saying to us, "Behold, the tabernacle of God is with men, and he will dwell with them, and they shall be his people, and God himself shall be with them, and be their God. And God shall wipe away all tears from their eyes; and there shall be no more death, neither sorrow, nor crying, neither shall there be any more pain: for the former things are passed away." (Rev. 21:3-4)

HIS

His stone am I, to set as He shall please,
In arch or vault or pediment,
In cornice or in frieze;
A pillar in His temple made,
Or in the lowly pavement laid,
The socket where a torch may rest,
Or jewel flashing on His breast.

He needs them all; each does His will;
Each has its purpose to fulfill.
The stones on which the walls are built,
Deep hidden out of sight,
Have honour as the airy spire
That springs to meet the light.
It matters not where I shall be,
So He doth set and polish me.[48]

24

LIVING STONES

When Solomon built the temple which was to be the dwelling place of the Lord of Hosts, he gave orders that all the stones required were to be completely prepared before the actual building began, so that the walls, white and shining, should rise in splendor amid reverent and majestic silence. "And the king commanded, and they brought great stones, costly stones, and hewed stones, to lay the foundation of the house. . . . And the house, when it was in building, was built of stone made ready before it was brought thither: so that there was neither hammer nor axe nor any tool of iron heard in the house, while it was in building." (1 Kings 5:17; 6:7)

The New Testament teaches that God's people are the stones which are built upon the foundation of Jesus Christ into a holy dwelling place for Him. "Ye are . . . the household of God; and are built upon the foundation of the apostles and prophets, Jesus Christ himself being the chief corner stone; in whom all the building fitly framed together groweth unto an holy temple in the Lord: in whom ye also are builded together for an habitation of God through the Spirit." "Ye also, as lively stones, are built up a spiritual house, an holy priesthood, to offer up spiritual sacrifices, acceptable to God by Jesus Christ." *(Eph. 2:19-22; 1 Pet. 2:5)*

If stones were sensate things, it would not be pleasant to be prepared for human use. To be blasted from their home in the rock; to be hewn into pieces; to have each piece chiseled and carved to certain specifications, then sanded and polished to perfection—yet that is the only way stones can be made into buildings for man. David, as well as his son Solomon, prepared stones for God's temple; we read that he prepared "onyx stones, and stones to be set, glistering stones, and of divers colours, and all manner of precious stones, and marble stones in abundance." Different stones would be perfected in different ways; but each, when the work was complete, would fill its own particular position and function in the builder's plan. *(1 Chron. 29:2)*

God is our Builder; the Architect of the universe is the great Designer both of the heavenly temple, of which we form a part, and of our individual lives. We are the stones of His choosing and His workmanship, and He has a plan and a particular use for each of us. We are of great variety, and the refinements that will make one stone ready and fit for use will not do for another, so we are individually perfected. Unlike earthly stones, we lively stones are sentient beings; we feel in our spirits, our minds, and sometimes in our bodies, the strokes of the hammer, the chisel, and the graving tool that shape us to our Master's design. Our uses are infinite in number and widely varying; and as we may not comprehend them in this life, neither can we understand the painful processes that prepare us for them. But we know that our destiny is eternal perfection in the pure presence of God: shall we then fear or draw back from the hand of Him who works all things after the counsel of His own will: that we should be to the praise of His glory? *(Eph. 1:11-12)*

Unlike earthly stones, we can resist the hand of the Builder upon us, can thwart His plan and mar His workmanship. He will shape other stones to His use if we will not let Him have

His way with us; His purposes will be fulfilled, but we ourselves shall suffer loss. How sad to suffer and not accomplish that eternal end for which the suffering was designed!

Writing to the Corinthian Christians, Paul used a slightly different imagery than that we have been considering. He saw us as builders, raising to God's glory a building of materials that must stand the test of the fire of His holiness, even while we ourselves are being shaped as lively stones for use in His temple. "We are labourers together with God: ye are God's husbandry, ye are God's building. . . . Other foundation can no man lay than that is laid, which is Jesus Christ. . . . Now if any man build upon this foundation gold, silver, precious stones, wood, hay, stubble; every man's work shall be made manifest: for the day shall declare it, because it shall be revealed by fire; and the fire shall try every man's work of what sort it is. . . . If any man's work shall be burned, he shall suffer loss: but he himself shall be saved; yet so as by fire. Know ye not that ye are the temple of God, and that the Spirit of God dwelleth in you?" (1 Cor. 3:9, 11-13, 15-16)

The way in which we accept the hedge that God has placed about us and cooperate with Him, as He seeks to shape our lives to fit us for our place and use in His eternal purpose, is one of the materials with which we must build to His glory. Will our response to His painful molding of our spirits be able to stand His test of fire in the day of revelation?

As living stones, we are being built by God into His temple; but He has also made us to be a holy priesthood to Himself, to offer up spiritual sacrifices to Him. From within the hedge where He has placed us, may we be enabled to offer to Him the acceptable sacrifices of love and obedience, submission and trust, patience and praise! (1 Pet. 2:5)

WITHIN THE HOLIEST

His priest am I, before Him day and night,
  Within His Holy Place;
And death, and life, and all things dark and bright,
  I spread before His face;
Rejoicing with His joy, yet ever still,
  For silence is my song;
My work, to bend beneath His blessed will,
  All day, and all night long—
Forever holding with Him converse sweet,
Yet speechless, for my gladness is complete.[44]

25

HE WORKETH

One of the sharpest thorns in the hedge of physical infirmity that surrounds so many of God's people is the fact that the restricted life it entails precludes much, even any, active Christian service. At home, the work of the Kingdom is crying for workers on every hand; afar, the whitened fields are crying for harvesters. Yet we hedge-dwellers, though feeling the burden and longing to take our place in the work force, are unable to do so. Because of the way we must live, we are likely to have more free time than most people; yet it must drain away in fruitless idleness, the hours filled with the unrewarding but inexorable necessities laid upon us by the nature of our infirmities.

"Then you can be a prayer warrior," our well-meaning but uninitiated friends declare roundly. "You can spend hours and hours interceding for those who are in the thick of the battle. Not many people have time enough to do that!" How unhappily such words jangle in our consciousness, building just one more barrier in that insurmountable wall of misunderstanding that lies between us and the rest of mankind! For no one knows like the sufferer just how much strength it takes to really pray, and how impossible it is for those with severe physical infirmities to summon enough mental energy and nervous stability to pray for more than a few minutes at a time. For most sufferers any degree of intense concentration and sustained mental effort is literally quite impossible; and the problem of how to maintain any sort of vital and workable relationship with God in the face of such a difficulty is the single greatest problem in the lives of suffering Christians. Just to exist and to do daily battle with this devitalizing and demoralizing situation is in itself a task calling for almost heroic effort, as only those who must live in this way can appreciate; and it takes all the strength we have. If even such elementary involvement in the things of the Kingdom is so difficult for us, how, then, are we to share in its work?

But our God does not leave His children without answers, even in such exigencies. The responsibility is His: "It is God which worketh in you both to will and to do of his good pleasures"; and He "worketh all things after the counsel of his own will." This work of faith goes on day and night, depending not on our strength, but upon His faithfulness. The burden, then, is not upon us, but upon Him; we may cast our burden upon the Lord and find that He does indeed sustain us. *(Phil. 2:13; Eph. 1:11)*

"What shall we do, that we might work the works of God?" Jesus was asked. He replied, "This is the work of God, that ye believe on him whom he hath sent." God's work is carried on not so much by what we do as by what we are. He works *in* us that which is well-pleasing in His sight, and then He works *through* us, according to the working whereby He is able even to subdue all things unto Himself, to bring about His purposes; but in both cases He does the work. And the amount of work He can do through us is in the direct proportion to the amount of work that we have allowed Him to do in us. *(John 6:28-29; Heb. 13:21; Phil. 3:21)*

And here it is that the Father speaks with particular tenderness and directness to those whose lives He has hedged in. By the very urgency of our necessities, we are thrown back on God in a significant way. In order to survive, we are forced to meet God face to face and come to terms with Him concerning the facts of our existence. In this way we may be compelled to allow Him to do a deeper work of faith and grace within us than we might be willing to let Him do if we enjoyed normal health and activities. This is not to say that other persons may not root their lives as deeply into God as those whose lives are hedged in; they may, and often they do. But the human tendency is to live and work in one's own strength; and to a greater or lesser extent, and often without knowing it, many sincere Christians do just that. We hedge-dwellers, however, can't live by ourselves, for we have insufficient strength to survive. We must come to God for grace to live this day, this hour, even this moment; and so God's work is done in us as our awful need drives us to Him in utter helplessness and forces us to live by His strength. This is what Paul meant when he said: "When I am weak, then am I strong"; and without weakness, God's strength cannot be perfected in us. May not our weakness, then, be the means by which our Father's purposes and work may be done in and through us? And need we then feel so useless as we see the whitened fields around us? For it is God who works; and if He is working in us, whether we can share in normal Christian activities or not, we may be sure that He is also working through us. (2 Cor. 12:10)

Just what the work is that He works through us may sometimes be discerned, or partially discerned, and sometimes be wholly hidden from our eyes. Fragmentary and disconnected as our prayers may be, we do pray, and God in His graciousness sometimes lets us see the outworking of His answers. There is likely to be a quiet ministry to others of our own kind—those of the hedged-in lives—and we "minister grace" each to the other. Sometimes the way in which God teaches us to live within our hedges constitutes a profound witness before those who understand most fully the difficulties under which we live—our medical advisors—and by us God does His work in them. Those of us who are able to work, no matter with what degree of difficulty, are often a powerful witness to our fellow workers, as the life of God shows out through our lives against heavy odds. The neighbors beside whom we live may see God's sustaining strength through us as we stand up to constant pain and pressure with patience and quiet assurance. Many a hedged-in Christian has learned to reach out to the world beyond by letters or other writing. Indeed, the great bulk of our New Testament consists of letters written by hedge-dwellers to their friends. And God's work has been done by the Word sent forth. So God does His work in us and through us; in ways visible and invisible, ceaselessly, constantly, triumphantly, "He worketh."

Someone has said that for every person who is tested by Satan and falls, God has His counterpart or counterparts somewhere who, though equally or even more bitterly tested, firmly stand, as a sign to the hosts of hell that the power of life and light in Christ Jesus is stronger than the power of death and darkness. Have you ever considered, you who suffer so fruitlessly, so long and so alone, that this may be your work for God in this life—to demonstrate His keeping power before the Prince of Darkness? What a high and awesome calling of God this is, chosen not by man but by God Himself! Then let patience have her perfect work, that you may be perfect and entire, wanting nothing; that you may stand perfect and complete in all the will of God. (James 1:4; Col. 4:12)

Rich are the words of promise that God has given to those who commit their way to Him and trust Him to do His work in and through them. We need not fear that He will be unable to do His work, for He works "according to the working of His mighty power, which he wrought in Christ, when he raised him from the dead, and set him at His own right hand in the heavenly places, far above all principality, and power, and might, and dominion, and every name that is named, not only in this world, but also in that which is to come." Nothing can stop His work from going forward, for "every purpose of the Lord shall be performed." His work will bring glory to God: "All thy works shall praise thee, O Lord." And we need not fear that He will not complete His work, for He who on earth was able to say," I have finished the work which thou gavest me to do," is the One who will perfect that which concerns us. (Eph. 1:19-21; Jer. 51:29; Ps. 145:10; John 17:4; Ps. 138:8)

"Those that dwelt among plants and hedges: there they dwelt with the king for his work." Deep in the midst of a chapter of endless and dry-as-dust genealogies, it pleased the Spirit of God to hide these lovely words. Was it that the unsuspecting hedge-dweller, plowing wearily but steadfastly through the seemingly uninspiring verses, should laugh aloud with delight when he stumbles upon them? For how richly they describe the life of one who must dwell among plants and hedges: "with the king" and "for his work"! God has not asked us to forego the joy of sharing in His work, even though He may have asked us to live within a debilitating hedge. There we may live with Him; and in us and through us, "He worketh." (1 Chron. 4:23)

MY GOD SHALL BE MY STRENGTH

Isaiah 49:5

My God shall be my strength
  Throughout my pilgrim way;
My sure defence, my guard, my guide,
    My shield and stay;
Secure in Him my heart is strong
And lifts aloft faith's triumph-song.

My God shall be my strength
  Though fierce may be the foe;
No hosts of hell my trusting soul
    Shall overthrow:
Through Christ I conquer: by His power
I triumph in the evil hour.

My God shall be my strength
  Though flesh and heart may fail;
O'er want and weakness by His might
    I shall prevail.
In Christ I triumph over pain
And rise to face the foe again.

My God shall be my strength
  In sorrow's bitter hour;
In loneliness and loss I plead
    His sovereign power.
No harm can pass His perfect will,
And in His love my heart is still.

My God shall be my strength
  When death shall press his claim,
When languishing in weakness lies
    This mortal frame:
Through Christ triumphant I shall rise
To sing His grace in Paradise.[1]

26

GOD OUR STRENGTH

Blessed be thou, Lord God of Israel our father, for ever and ever. Thine, O Lord, is the greatness, and the power, and the glory, and the victory, and the majesty: for all that is in the heaven and in the earth is thine; thine is the kingdom, O Lord, and thou art exalted as head above all. Both riches and honour come of thee, and thou reignest over all; and in thine hand is power and might; and in thine hand it is to make great, and to give strength unto all. Now therefore, our God, we thank thee, and praise thy glorious name. (1 Chron. 29:10-13)

Only those who are denied it can truly appreciate the great blessing of a normal endowment of physical energy. The average person awakens feeling able to do his day's work and usually enjoys it; he comes home weary and refreshes himself by engaging in some activity quite different from his work and then is restored in sleep. Occasional vacations entailing a change of scene and pace bring him pleasure and renewed vigor. He may become ill, but usually he recovers quickly, and his illnesses are seldom severe enough or last long enough to drain his reservoir of strength.

Those beset with a hedge of physical infirmity, however, know little of such blessings. Theirs are nights of waking or broken, restless sleep; the new day begins as wearily as the old one ended. Whatever the tasks of the day, there is seldom enough energy to perform them even in a mediocre way, and joy in accomplishment is as rarely experienced as is pleasurable relaxation. Rest brings little restoration, and changes of scene are either impossible or else so complicate the physical situation that little benefit can be derived from the vacation. Pain is ever present, siphoning away what energy there is. And the debility is chronic, often stretching from childhood far into the future, broken only by sharp bouts of severe illness. Moreover, the situation is real: it does not exist only in the mind of the sufferer, but for a variety of reasons may be both real and incurable. Added to the problem, and often even more painful to bear, are the misunderstandings, the criticisms, the well-intentioned but totally wrong judgments passed upon the sufferer by those who are well; not to mention the worries, the fears, the loneliness, the depressions, and the economic difficulties that accompany such types of illness. Such a hedge is thorny indeed; yet thousands of people must live out their lives in just such circumstances. Where can they find strength to face the future—even the now?

Our God is a God of strength, and He has promised to give His strength to His people. Our part is simply to bring our weakness to Him in faith and to seek the Lord and His strength continually. As we do, we shall find that although our ailing bodies and weary spirits may fail us, God Himself will increasingly become the strength of our hearts and our portion forever; and in the depths of our being we shall come to know the truth of the psalmist's cry, "Blessed is the man whose strength is in thee!" (Ps. 29:11; 1 Chron. 16:11; Pss. 73:26; 84:5)

The Scriptures are strong with the strength of God, and a

few hours spent with a concordance in contemplation of that many-faceted strength will provide a reservoir for needy souls. The King of Glory is the Lord, strong and mighty in battle. He is clothed with strength, and His strength is everlasting; we are enjoined to trust in it forever. His is the strength of height and depth; the strength of the hills is His also. Both Job and Solomon saw His strength as being joined with His wisdom, counsel, and understanding: our strong Redeemer exercises His strength on His people's behalf with divine sovereignty, infinite compassion, and perfect wisdom that knows the end from the beginning and knows that his way is right. Of such a God as this, the trusting heart may truly exclaim: "O Lord God of hosts, who is a strong Lord like unto thee? or to thy faithfulness round about thee?" *(Ps. 24:8; Isa. 26:4; Pss. 68:34; 95:4; Job. 12:13; Prov. 8:14; Jer. 50:34; Ps. 89:8)*

God wants His people to learn to renew their strength in His. His eyes run to and fro over the earth seeking those who need Him, that He may show Himself strong on the behalf of those whose hearts are one with His; and He seeks to use His great power not to inveigh against our weakness and our failures, but to strengthen us. As we learn to wait before Him in the silence of worship and acceptance of His will, we shall find that our strength is renewed. *(Isa. 41:1; 2 Chron. 16:9; Job 23:6)*

God has given special promises of strength for those who must suffer pain and illness. He has promised to strengthen those who are sick, even to strengthen them on the bed of their languishing. He has covenanted His own unwearying power to those who are faint and increased strength to those who have no might. He has apportioned the measure of their strength, and He urges them to take hold of His strength to make up their lack, that they may be enabled to walk up and down in His name, spiritually if not always physically. He has told them that as they wait upon Him in quietness and confidence, their strength will be renewed—that as they learn to sit still before Him, they will find that His joy becomes their strength.

Truly, there is no lack to them that fear Him! (*Ezek. 34:16; Ps. 41:3; Isa. 40:28-31; Ps. 68:28; Isa. 27:5; Zech. 10:12; Isa. 30:15; 30:7; Neh. 8:10; Ps. 34:9*)

God has promised to provide a strong shelter for His children, and this shelter is none other than Himself. He is a strength to the needy in distress, a refuge from the storm, a shadow from the heat. He is our refuge and strength, a present help in time of trouble. He has given His name to be a strong tower into which His people may run and be safe. And as we shelter ourselves more and more deeply in God, we shall find strength for our daily needs. (*Isa. 25:4; Ps. 46:1; Prov. 18:10*)

Fear of the future is part of the burden of those who must suffer prolonged physical weakness, but far into the future shines the glory of the promises of God. "Thy shoes shall be iron and brass; and as thy days, so shall thy strength be," He has told us. He has promised to lead us in the way of His choosing, and the way of the Lord, though it may seem dark to us, is strength to the upright. As long as we live, we shall continue to find that our God will be our strength. (*Deut. 33:25; Prov. 10:29; Isa. 49:5*)

God teaches His children that human strength offers less security than spiritual strength, for the weakness of God is stronger than men's strength, and His strength is perfected in our weakness. No man will prevail by mortal strength, He tells us, but we are able to do all things through the strengthening of Christ. The race is not won by the swift, nor the battle by the strong, but by the power of God those who stumble are girded with strength. Mighty men are not delivered by much strength, but Scriptural story abounds with the exploits of those "who through faith ... out of weakness were made strong." Since God is the God of our strength, why should even the weakest of saints go mourning because of the oppression of the enemy of his soul? (*1 Cor. 1:25; 2 Cor. 12:9; 1 Sam. 2:9; Phil. 4:13; Eccles. 9:11; 1 Sam. 2:4; Ps. 33: 16; Heb. 11:33-34; Ps. 43:2*)

Paul tells us one reason why God allows the pressures of

weakness to bear down on us. "We were pressed out of measure, above strength," he writes, "... that we should not trust in ourselves, but in God." As long as we have one ounce of our own strength in which to trust, our human hearts will place our confidence there, even though we sometimes do it unconsciously; but God wants us to prove Him, to be strengthened with all might by His Spirit according to His glorious power. When we truly realize that it is God who has girded us for the battles of life, we are able to cry exultantly, "O my soul, thou hast trodden down strength!" for we know that in Him we have not only strength for our needs, but strength to spare. And it is so that His people may glorify Him in learning these truths and living triumphantly by His power that He sometimes takes our human strength away. (2 Cor. 1:8-9; Col. 1:11; Eph. 3:16; 2 Sam. 22:40; Judg. 5:21)

When we have learned to exchange our weakness for His strength and have proved it to be all-sufficient, we will be able to sing aloud to God, sharing in the triumphant song of those who have made the same discovery: "The Lord is my light and my salvation; whom shall I fear? the Lord is the strength of my life; of whom shall I be afraid?" "The Lord is my strength and my shield ... therefore my heart greatly rejoiceth; and with my song will I praise Him." "The Lord Jehovah is my strength and my song"; "I will love thee, O Lord, my strength." (Pss. 81:1; 27:1; 28:7; Isa. 12:2; Ps. 18:1)

We who know so little of earthly strength, have we so much to fear? God has made provision for His children, and "to them that have no might he increaseth strength." (Isa. 40:29)

THY NAME, O CHRIST

Thy Name, O Christ, as incense streaming forth,
 Sweetens our names before God's holy face;
Luring us from the south and from the north
  Unto the sacred place.

In Thee God's promise is Amen and Yea.
 What art Thou to us? Prize of every lot;
Shepherd and Door, our Life, our Truth, our Way—
  Nay, Lord, what art Thou not?[18]

27

PRECIOUS NAME

His name shall endure for ever: his name shall be continued as long as the sun: and men shall be blessed in him: all nations shall call him blessed. Blessed be the Lord God, the God of Israel, who only doeth wondrous things. And blessed be his glorious name for ever; and let the whole earth be filled with his glory; Amen, and Amen. (Ps. 72: 17-19)

One of the surest means by which the weak and needy may be made strong is by drawing upon the strength of the holy name of God.

Anything like an adequate consideration of the name and names of God is far too exhaustive to include here; a few hours spent with any good concordance can open the door to untold riches of grace and strength for any who seek it—a wealth more than sufficient for our every need. However, let us consider, even if all too briefly, something of the balm and blessing that may be found in the contemplation of the precious name of our Lord.

Throughout the Scriptures, God revealed Himself to His people in the names by which He chose to be called. His character, His nature, His will, His faithfulness, His might, His honor, His renown, His glory, His grace, His love—all that He is in Himself and in His attributes was disclosed by His name. His name was varied from time to time, as He had occasion to reveal Himself to His people in different capacities; over two hundred titles are used in the Scriptures. A list of His names should have a prominent place in the armory of every Christian and the appropriate name be invoked in any time of need. To call on the name of the Lord is to invoke His very Self, for "as his name is, so is he." (1 Sam. 25:25)

God set His name as a seal upon His people: He chose them that they might be unto Him "for a people, and for a name, and for a praise, and for a glory." He "led them ... with his glorious arm . . . to make himself an everlasting name." Likewise He set His name upon Zion: "I have chosen to set my name there" and upon the Temple: "this house ... I have hallowed for my name." Israel was faithless to His name times without number and was scattered in exile; Zion was destroyed and the Temple desecrated; but always there was the promise of forgiveness and restoration, of renewal and eventual regathering and total redemption, because of the holy name— "for his name's sake." Once God had set His name upon something, He could never cast it off, but was pledged by Himself to love it and care for it unendingly and eventually to redeem it totally. "He abideth faithful: he cannot deny himself." (Jer. 13:11; Isa. 63:12; Neh. 1:9; 1 Kings 9:7; Ps. 23:3; 2 Tim. 2:13)

God has set His name upon every believer in the Lord Jesus Christ, so that we, too, rest enclosed in God's faithfulness to His own name. "I am called by thy name, O Lord God of hosts." "Thou, O Lord, art in the midst of us, and we are called by thy name." What a refuge and strength is the name of our God! Shall we not, then, learn to live in its power? (Jer. 15:16; 14:9)

God's name is an inexhaustible number of things to His people, embracing every need known to the human heart. It is not possible to list here the names by which He loves to call Himself, but he is a wise Christian who finds out what they are and learns to bring his needs to that limitless source of supply. He who will not take time to discover the names of his God need not wonder if he has little sense of His presence or seldom experiences His deliverance.

Sweetest among all the myriad names of God is His name of redeeming love, Jehovah-Jesus: "Jesus ... (who) shall save his people from their sins"; "Emmanuel ... God with us." Upon His shoulder shall be the government of all the universe and of all the details of our individual, hedged-in lives: "His name shall be called Wonderful, Counsellor, The mighty God, The everlasting Father, The Prince of Peace," and "of the increase of his government and peace there shall be no end." His is the name which is above every name before whom every knee shall one day bow, that holy name that shall one day be written in the foreheads of those who walk with Him in white in the heavenly Jerusalem. His is the name as ointment poured forth that breathes its balm in sorrow, relieves our pain, and lightens our burdens; His the mighty name before which devils fall and flee and the Accuser is cast down. His is the name in which our prayers are heard and answered, by which the Comforter, the Holy Spirit, is sent to teach us of the things of God to bring the strength of His word to our failing remembrance. Let us learn to lay it on our hearts in grace and power, to live in its healing strength when our scant store is spent, and to triumph over the Evil One in its might. And while Jesus may always be the first and dearest name of God to the Christian, let us seek to learn His many Old Testament names as well, for each fresh revelation of the Father shows us ever more deeply and clearly the glories of our Savior, who "was in the beginning with God," and who "was God." (*Matt. 1:21,23; Isa. 9:6-7; Phil. 2:9; Rev. 22:4; Song of Sol. 1:3; John 1:1-2*)

The name of God is victory to those who trust in it: "The name of the Lord is a strong tower: the righteous runneth into

it, and is safe"; "Through thee will we push down our enemies: through thy name will we tread them under." "In the
name of our God we will set up our banners. . . . some trust in
chariots, and some in horses: but we will remember the name
of the Lord our God." "They that know thy name will put
their trust in thee." *(Prov. 18:10; Pss. 44:5; 20:5, 7; 9:10)*

God has promised deliverance to those who know His
name: "Because he hath set his love upon me, therefore will I
deliver him: I will set him on high, because he hath known my
name. He shall call upon me, and I will answer him: I will be
with him in trouble; I will deliver him, and honour him. With
long life will I satisfy him, and shew him my salvation." *(Ps.
91:14-16)*

God has particular blessings for those who love His name
and meditate upon it: "They that feared the Lord spake often
one to another: and the Lord hearkened, and heard it, and a
book of remembrance was written before him for them that
feared the Lord, and that thought upon his name. And they
shall be mine, saith the Lord of hosts, in that day when I make
up my jewels; and I will spare them, as a man spareth his own
son that serveth him." *(Mal. 3:16-17)*

God has commanded joy for those who trust His name:
"Let all those that put their trust in thee rejoice: let them ever
shout for joy, because thou defendest them: let them also that
love thy name be joyful in thee." *(Ps. 5:11)*

God has not exempted those who know His name from
suffering; rather, He warns us that suffering is the lot of those
who are faithful to His name. Speaking of the newly converted Saul of Tarsus, He disclosed His purpose for his life: "He is
a chosen vessel unto me, to bear my name before the Gentiles,
and kings, and the children of Israel. For I will shew him how
great things he must suffer for my name's sake." And the early
apostles suffered gladly, "rejoicing that they were counted
worthy to suffer shame for his name." But He has promised
that the victors shall be rewarded by an ever-increasing knowledge of that name: "Him that overcometh will I make a pillar

in the temple of my God, and he shall go no more out: and I will write upon him the name of my God, and the name of the city of my God, which is new Jerusalem, which cometh down out of heaven from my God: and I will write upon him my new name." *(Acts 9:15; 5:41; Rev. 3:12)*

"Thou hast given me the heritage of those that fear thy name," cried the Psalmist, and what a heritage it is! How shall we think upon it but with thanksgiving and with total acceptance of all that God may choose to give with it! "Hallowed be thy name" must be our response to His will for us, no matter how sharp the thorns of the hedge He has placed about us. "All people will walk every one in the name of his god, and we will walk in the name of the Lord our God for ever and ever." *(Ps. 61:5; Matt. 6:9; Mic. 4:5)*

May all the desire of our souls, then, be to His name and to the remembrance of Him. Let us seek to wait on His name, knowing it is good; to remember His name in the darkness of our night and keep His law; to sing praise to His name and to exalt His name together. Let us continually rest on Him, knowing that it is in His name that we go against the multitude of difficulties that beset us. Let us beseech Him constantly to unite our fragmented hearts to fear His name; and let us remember that no matter how distant we may feel Him to be at any particular time, His name is always near. Blessed be his glorious name forever! *(Isa. 26:8; Pss. 52:9; 119:55; 9:2; 34:3; 2 Chron. 14:11; Pss. 86:11; 75:1)*

WE ARE THE LORD'S

We are the Lord's: His all-sufficient merit
Sealed on the cross, to us this grace accords;
We are the Lord's, and all things shall inherit:
Whether we live or die, we are the Lord's.

We are the Lord's: then let us gladly tender
Our souls to Him in deeds, not empty words;
Let heart, and tongue, and life, combine to render
No doubtful witness that we are the Lord's.

We are the Lord's: no darkness brooding o'er us
Can make us tremble, whilst this star affords
A steady light along the path before us—
Faith's full assurance that we are the Lord's.

We are the Lord's: no evil can befall us
In the dread hour of life's fast loosening cords;
No pangs of death shall even then appall us;
Death we shall vanquish, for we are the Lord's.[40]

28

BY LIFE OR BY DEATH

*Christ shall be magnified in my body, whether it be by life,
or by death. For to me to live is Christ, and to die is gain.*
(Phil. 1:20-21)

We humans tend to think that our bodies are our own
personal property; but such is not the teaching of the New
Testament, as Paul makes clear: "What? know ye not that
your body is the temple of the Holy Ghost which is in you,
which ye have of God, and ye are not your own? For ye are
bought with a price: therefore glorify God in your body, and
in your spirit, which are God's." Again he writes: "I beseech
you therefore, brethren, by the mercies of God, that ye present
your bodies a living sacrifice, holy, acceptable unto God, which
is your reasonable service." (1 Cor. 6:19-20; Rom. 12:1)

Our redeemed bodies are meant to be instruments of God's
praise and glory, and we are urged to yield them to Him for
this purpose.

This has a particular significance for the sufferer. It is one
thing to glorify God in a body consecrated to His service and
active in His work; it is quite another to be willing to glorify

Him in bodily suffering, even in death. Yet the Scriptures make it plain that for some of God's children it is in this way, and in this way alone, that He must be glorified.

His own Son had to glorify the Father in this way. "When he cometh into the world, he saith, Sacrifice and offering thou wouldest not, but a body hast thou prepared me. . . . Then said I, Lo, I come . . . to do thy will, O God." (Heb. 10:5,7)

Christ was born into the human family with a body like ours, and He lived in that body for thirty-three years, subject to all the bodily temptations, restraints, and disciplines that we experience. In that body He suffered, knowing hunger, thirst, privation, weariness, and pain beyond description, even death by torture. He who had inhabited the limitless freedoms of Eternity glorified God within the petty restrictions of human life; He who was Life itself glorified God in the throes of human death and more—for He tasted the bitterness of eternal death for us, which is something we shall never have to do. In infinite condescension, the Lord Jesus glorified God in His body by life and by death.

The Gospel of John gives us three outstanding instances of suffering being not only permitted, but actually designed, that God might be glorified.

John 9 tells the story of the man born blind, groping in darkness from infancy to maturity that one shining, holy day he might be the instrument of God's glory. When, after the manner of the time, the disciples asked whose sin had caused such suffering, the Master replied that the blindness was not the result of the man's own sin, nor that of his parents, but that the works of God should be revealed through him. Then Christ went on to make the great declaration, "I am the light of the world," and proved it by dispelling forever the darkness of the man who had suffered a lifetime of blindness for just this moment of God's revelation; and we read that as a result, he believed on the Savior and worshiped him. (John 9:5)

John 11 brings us the familiar tale of Lazarus, whom Jesus loved. In Larazus' home in Bethany welcome always awaited

Him, and there He loved to visit. When word was brought to the Savior, "Lord, behold, he whom thou lovest is sick," Jesus answered, "This sickness is not unto death, but for the glory of God, that the Son of God might be glorified thereby," and then made no move to heal Lazarus, or even to set out for Bethany until four days after his friend's death and burial. And even after His arrival, Jesus seemed to spend a surprisingly long time in conversation before doing anything to help. "I am glad for your sakes that I was not there," He told His disciples, preparing them for His own death so soon to follow, "to the intent ye may believe." Then before the assembled crowd He made the glorious affirmation whose truth has cheered sorrowing hearts ever since: "I am the resurrection, and the life: he that believeth in me, though he were dead, yet shall he live: and whosoever liveth and believeth in me shall never die." Finally He proved His power over death by calling Lazarus back to life; and we read that as a result, many believed on him. *(John 11:3-4, 15, 25-26)*

In John 21 we find Jesus somewhat obliquely telling Peter something of what awaited him in the future. We read: "This spake he, signifying by what death he should glorify God." History bore out the truth of His words: for not only Peter, but almost all of Christ's disciples were called upon to glorify God by violent and terrible deaths; but the Gospel has spread around the globe as a result. *(John 21:19)*

And so John shows us a congenital illness followed many years later by healing; a sickness unto death in which death was finally conquered; and the foreshadowing of a death where the Prince of Darkness was allowed, from a human point of view, to triumph: and all are for one reason—that God might be glorified, whether by life or by death.

The sole reason for our existence in this body is that God may be glorified in us—in these frail, sensitive, pain-prone bodies in which we must serve Him on earth. We may live surrounded by a hedge of suffering from infancy and, unlike the man born blind, may never be granted healing. Like

Lazarus, we may be struck down by sudden disaster in mid-life and suffer and die without the Savior coming to our physical aid, even with the very heavens in which we have trusted silent and seemingly deaf to our cries. Or like Peter, we may live a long and active life in God's service, only to suffer apparent desertion and horror in old age. Are we willing to offer our bodies to God for His glory and to take what He sends us without flinching, until we can say at last, "I have glorified thee on the earth: I have finished the work which thou gavest me to do"? His word to those who are willing to turn life's pain into a vehicle for His glory will be, "Fear none of those things which thou shalt suffer . . . be thou faithful unto death, and I will give thee a crown of life." For "neither death, nor life . . . shall be able to separate us from the love of God, which is in Christ Jesus our Lord" (John 17:4; Rev. 2:10; Rom. 8:38-39)

Suffering and death will come to all of us, whether we will or not; suffering and death for the glory of God come only to those who give their bodies to God, that through them He may be glorified. How sad to suffer, even to die, and not win the crown!

The suffering or death that God sends into our lives to display His glory may not necessarily be our own; it may be that of someone dearer to us than life itself. God asked glory of this sort of the prophet Ezekiel. "The word of the Lord came unto me, saying, Son of man, behold, I take away from thee the desire of thine eyes with a stroke: yet neither shalt thou mourn nor weep, neither shall thy tears run down. Forbear to cry, make no mourning for the dead, bind the (at)tire of thine head upon thee, and put on thy shoes upon thy feet, and cover not thy lips, and eat not the bread of men. So I spake unto the people in the morning; and at evening my wife died; and I did in the morning as I was commanded." Not only did Ezekiel suffer the loss of his beloved wife, but he was forbidden to show grief in any way; he was commanded to carry on with his daily routine as though nothing had happened—an unusual and incredibly difficult thing to be asked to do, surely! Yet because of his obedience God's word was made plain to the people: "Thus Ezekiel is unto you a sign: according to all that he hath done shall ye do: and when this cometh, ye shall know that I am the Lord." And so God's will for Israel was done, His glory shown by Ezekiel both by life and by death. (Ezek. 24:15-18, 24)

To the Christian, neither life nor death can hold any real terrors. Our Savior is He who says to us: "Fear not; I am the first and the last: I am he that liveth, and was dead; and, behold, I am alive for evermore, Amen; and have the keys of hell and of death." "For all things are yours," wrote the triumphant Paul, "whether . . . the world, or life, or death, or things present, or things to come; all are yours; and ye are Christ's; and Christ is God's." What can we fear in the face of assurance like this? (Rev. 1:17-18; 1 Cor. 3:21-23)

Alexander Whyte used to exhort his parishioners to "make your deathbed every day that you live," that God might not be robbed of His glory in the sudden approach of an evil hour for which no preparation had ever been made.

"I am now ready to be offered, and the time of my departure is at hand," wrote Paul to Timothy not long before his death by martyrdom. "I have fought a good fight, I have finished my course, I have kept the faith: henceforth there is laid up for me a crown of righteousness, which the Lord, the righteous judge, shall give me at that day." (2 Tim. 4:6-8)

May we, too, at the end be able to say:

> Yea, through life, death, through sorrow and through sinning,
> He shall suffice me, for He hath sufficed:
> Christ is the end, for Chirst was the beginning;
> Christ the beginning, for the end is Christ.[2]

How gloriously God's true saints know how to die!

FOLLOW THOU ME

Lord, carry me.—Nay, but I grant thee strength
To walk and work thy way to Heaven at length.—

Lord, why then am I weak?—Because I give
Power to the weak, and bid the dying live.—

Lord, I am tired.—He hath not much desired
The goal who at the starting-point is tired.—

Lord, dost Thou know?—I know what is in man;
What the flesh can, and what the spirit can.—

Lord, dost Thou care?—Yea, for thy gain or loss
So much I cared, it brought Me to the Cross.—

Lord, I believe; help Thou mine unbelief.—
Good is the word; but rise, for life is brief.—

The follower is not greater than the Chief:
Follow thou Me along My way of grief.[18]

29

TO HIM THAT OVERCOMETH

We Christians are sometimes tempted to think that God requires a great deal of His people in asking them to be faithful to Him throughout much unexplained suffering. We quite forget that non-Christians likewise find their lives overshadowed by sorrows for which there seem to be no good reasons; Christians and non-Christians alike are partakers of a common heritage of human pain. We who know the Savior have the assurance that while we may not now understand the reason for our suffering, yet there is a reason, and we trust that one day God will make it plain to us. Because we know the nature of our God, we know that that reason, whatever it is, is good; and in the strength of that assurance we live from day to day, trusting God to care for us both now and hereafter. Moreover, we know that our Savior Himself partook of our pain to the utmost and beyond; and we have His presence with us to sustain us and give us strength to endure.

God does, indeed, ask His saints to endure and suffer many things: tribulation, hardness, affliction, chastening, temptation, misunderstanding, persecution, shame, need, reproach, loss, to name but a few. But He has also told us that if we endure to the end we shall be saved, and that if we suffer with Him we shall also reign with Him. So our darkness is shot through with promise of glory that non-Christians in their sorrow can never know. (1 Thess. 3:4; 2 Tim. 2:3; 3:12; 4:5; Heb. 12:7; 13:3; James 1:12; 1 Pet. 2:19; Phil. 4:12; 3:8; Acts 5:41; Matt. 24:13; 2 Tim. 2:12)

But our gracious Father has done infinitely more for His children. As if it were not enough that we should have hope of eternal salvation and eventual knowledge of the "why" of human pain, He has promised specific rewards to those who overcome in their suffering and are faithful to Him to the end.

In the second and third chapters of Revelation the Spirit pictures in seven-fold glory the rewards God has reserved in heaven for His overcomers. He promises that He will give the overcomer to eat of the tree of life in the midst of the paradise of God, and he will not be hurt in the second death. He will eat of the hidden manna and receive a white stone wherein is written a new name, known only to himself and to God. He will be given power and rule over the nations, and for his sceptre he will have the morning star. He will be clothed in white raiment, and the Savior will confess his name before the Father and His angels. He will be made a pillar in the temple of God, from which he will nevermore go out; and the name of God and the New Jerusalem and the name of the Redeemer Himself will be written upon him. He will sit with Christ in His Throne, even as Christ overcame and shares the Throne of His Father. What an inheritance of unimaginable glory awaits those who have overcome the thorns of earth's hedge! Truly, "He that overcometh shall inherit all things; and I will be his God, and he shall be my son." (Rev. 2:7, 11, 17, 26-28; 3:5, 12, 21; 21:7)

Nor is that all: God has also promised that there will be crowns for those who are faithful to the end in enduring temptation—the unfading crowns of life, glory, and righteousness. (Rev. 2:10; James 1:12; 1 Pet. 5:4; 2 Tim. 4:8)

What can one say to words such as these? To think that in

addition to giving us the blessings of salvation, eternal life, and His realized presence with us in our trials here and now, the Father should reward His children in such incredible measure, simply for standing up to the vicissitudes of human life with a strength of spirit that is often matched and sometimes even surpassed by others who must suffer alone and without hope! Only our tears can express the love and gratitude called forth by such kingly grace.

Just what form these promised rewards will take, who can tell? Sufficient to know that if they are not as lovely and satisfying as these specific words imply, then they will be something infinitely better and more beautiful, something for which no earthly words or symbols exist, and hence indescribable and inconceivable to us now. The fruit of the tree of life, the hidden manna—what food that will be for souls that hunger and thirst for God! The white stone, with the new and secret name known only to God and the soul that receives it—what infinite value our God must set on individuality of personality to know each one of His overcomers so personally and so intimately! The white raiment, forever spotless—what a joy after this life of soiling and defeat! The pillar eternally erect—what a strength after this pilgrimage of weakness and failure! To receive the morning star, sweet synonym for the Savior's own person; to be given the holy name of God Himself and the name of His city and the new name of the Lamb—only a God like ours could have designed rewards such as these! And only the Head that was crowned with thorns could fashion such crowns of life, righteousness, and glory— part of Himself bestowed eternally upon His faithful over- comers. What can we do but fall down before Him who sits upon the throne and worship Him for ever and ever; with all the hosts of heaven to cast our crowns before His feet and cry, "Thou art worthy, O Lord. . . . Worthy is the Lamb that was slain to receive power, and riches, and wisdom, and strength, and honour, and glory, and blessing. . . . Blessing, and honour, and glory, and power, be unto him that sitteth upon the throne, and unto the Lamb for ever and ever." (Rev. 22:16; 4:11; 5:12,13)

Then should we not bow in His presence with hearts of burning adoration, seeking His grace to be faithful to Him in whatever He may ask of us, that we may triumph over the evils of our hedge and appear before Him as overcomers in that day? May it be said of us:

"These are they which came out of great tribulation, and have washed their robes, and made them white in the blood of the Lamb. Therefore are they before the throne of God, and serve Him day and night in his temple: and he that sitteth upon the throne shall dwell among them. They shall hunger no more, neither thirst any more; neither shall the sun light on them, nor any heat. For the Lamb which is in the midst of the throne shall feed them, and shall lead them unto living waters: and God shall wipe away all tears from their eyes." (Rev. 7:14-17)

Is any road too long, too hard, that leads to this?

THE CITY OF GOD

City of God, how brightly shines
 Thy glory on my way!
The pilgrim path of earth I tread
Blessed by thy radiance round my head,
 And guided by thy ray.

City of God, how sweet thou art,
 How true, how dear, how fair!
In thee is all my soul's delight,
In thee my rest, my strength, my right,
 And all my trust is there.

City of God, from out thy throne
 Life's boundless river flows;
There is my cleansing, there my peace,
There is my healing, pain's surcease,
 And balm for all earth's woes.

City of God, I long to stand
 Upon thy shining shore;
To drink thy clear and crystal tide
Till, with thy fullness satisfied,
 My soul shall thirst no more!

City of God, my heart's desire,
 Home of my spirit, thou
My final consummation art:
Yet, dwelling in the Saviour's heart,
 I may possess thee now.

O New Jerusalem, thou art here!
 I dwell this day in thee,
Drawing my life, my love, my all,
From Him who built thy jasper wall—
 For thou art none but He![1]

30

TAKE HEAVEN

I salute you. I am your friend, and my love for you goes deep.
There is nothing I can give you which you have not already;
but there is much, very much, which though I cannot give it,
you can take. No heaven can come to us unless our hearts
find rest in it today. Take heaven. No peace lies in the future
which is not hidden in this precious little instant. Take
peace. The gloom of the world is but a shadow. Behind it,
yet within our reach, is joy. There is radiance and courage
in the darkness could we but see; and to see, we have only
to look. Life is so generous a giver, but we, judging its gifts
by their coverings, cast them away as ugly or heavy or hard.
Remove the covering, and you will find beneath it a living
splendor, woven of love, and wisdom, and power. Welcome
it, greet it, and touch the angel's hand that brings it.

Everything we call a trial, a sorrow, a duty: believe me, that
angel's hand is there, the gift is there, and the wonder of an
overshadowing Presence. Our joys, too: be not content with
them as joys. They, too, conceal diviner gifts. Life is so full
of meaning and purpose, so full of beauty beneath its covering, that you will find earth but cloaks your heaven. Courage,
then, to claim it, that is all! But courage you have, and the

*knowledge that we are pilgrims wending through unknown
country our way home.*

These words, written in a letter of Christmas greeting by
Giovanni da Fiesole (Fra Angelico, 1387–1455), contain
some profound truth, possibly none of which is more searching
than his words about heaven: "No heaven can come to us
unless our hearts find rest in it today."

God has disclosed that His ultimate purpose for every Christian is nothing less than an eternity spent in His own presence.
At many points in Scripture the dark clouds that gather about
the unfolding story of man's flight from God are suddenly shot
through with flashes of the glory that is to be revealed. Here
and there the prophets break their pronouncements of the evil
brought about by sin to envisage, in blazing flights of sublime
language, redemption's final consummation; and cold indeed is
the Christian whose heart is not kindled to burn with renewed
love towards his God as he reads them.

But how often do most Christians contemplate the heavenly
glory? Alas, all too seldom; possibly not at all. If we think on
heaven, it is as something nebulous and afar, approachable
only through death, which is something we do not like to
consider. Few of us have learned the secret of which Fra
Angelico wrote so warmly—that heaven is not only for the
future, but for now, for this present moment; and it is meant
to bless our path and be a source of strength and repose to us
today.

Certain and lovely as the future blessings of heaven are,
they are not the only reason we should learn to visit heaven
and to drink deeply of its delights. There is comfort in the
knowledge that sickness, sorrow, and all the other painful
effects of sin on the human spirit will one day be no more, but
this is only a small part of what heaven should mean to the
pilgrim heart. The deepest joys of heaven are those which can
bless us now, from which we can draw strength to live triumphantly today; and to no one may heaven be more nourish-

ing and real than to those who have had to live their earthly lives within one of God's hedges. It is for present blessing and strength to overcome that we should contemplate heaven.

Heaven is essentially the enjoyment of the pure presence of God in all His perfection. It is being at home in the deepest and sweetest sense. It is vision that sees all of time as being caught up inextricably in the perfect whole of God's timeless plan. It is the perfect freedom from care that is the result of adequate and unfailing supply. It is worship; it is adoration; it is praise. It is the total fusion of the soul with God.

True, it is more; we are promised endless delights of which we may not partake until we arrive, fully redeemed, at that holy and blessed estate. But the truest essence of heaven may be enjoyed now, and it is on the tasting of its present joys that we should set our hearts and minds. Sinful and earthbound as we are, we may not drink as deeply of the fullness of God now as we shall when forever freed from sin, but we may drink of Him far more deeply than most of us do; and herein lies the point of Angelico's Christmas admonition: "Take heaven."

Can a soul that does not actively live in the light of the joys of heaven here enjoy them completely when he reaches heaven? Can the pure presence of God be truly a joy to one who has not consciously and deliberately practiced that presence on earth? Granted that we shall then be perfected, and that the state of the blessed is shrouded in mystery which the human mind cannot penetrate; but it would seem reasonable to suppose that the soul who has most fully enjoyed his God here will know the deepest enjoyment in heaven. And even if God has some way of equalizing such things, it is quite certain that the soul who here knows God most truly will know more of heaven on earth than those who live less in His presence; and that in itself is a prize worth striving for, even if no other heaven existed.

But heaven is real; and here is where pain may prove to be a messenger of God Himself on behalf of heaven. If it is true that in heaven each soul will be filled with God's fullness to capacity, so that all will know perfect satisfaction, is it not also true that the soul with the greater capacity will receive more of God? Surely such is the teaching of the gospel writers, with their emphasis on spiritual rewards, their warnings about works that will not stand and souls that will be saved, as if by fire, but shall suffer loss. We are urged to strive for the mastery, to build with imperishable materials, to reach for the crown of eternal enjoyment, and to enlarge our capacity on earth that we may be capable of receiving greater joys in heaven.

If there is one thing that pain or sorrow will do for a Christian, it is to enlarge his capacity for God. In the desperation of our need we reach out for Him; we throw ourselves upon His mercy and cling to Him in our helplessness. In doing so, are we not being prepared, all unwittingly, to enjoy more completely the joys of heaven—in effect, to "take heaven" now? The highest joys of heaven and earth are one: the knowledge and enjoyment of God Himself. As we are forced by our hedges to let the things of earth fall away and to open our hearts more and more widely to the comforts and joys of God, are we not now entering into the joys of heaven? And is it not true, in a sense, that "no heaven can come to us unless our hearts find rest in it today"?

Pain, then, may prepare us for heaven, but such alchemy is far from automatic. To make effective use of pain as a means of laying up treasure in heaven calls for resolute and active participation on the part of the sufferer. Pain in itself is a sterile thing, but, like the plow that bites deep into the winter-bound earth releasing life-giving nutrients and allowing sun and air and rain to penetrate, pain can prepare the way for fruitfulness. The rest is up to us. We all know those, even Christians, who have let their pain and sorrow make them hard and bitter or querulous and critical. Pain may be God's messenger, but it is we who must see to it that we allow it to do God's work in our lives; and as we reach out to God for help in this endeavor, His grace will flood towards us like a river from a newly opened dam.

How does this come about? "Take heaven," wrote Fra Angelico simply. We set our hearts, minds, and affections on things above, not on things on the earth. We refuse to allow the present scene to blot out the reality of the invisible; we keep our eyes turned toward the Lord, and our windows open "toward Jerusalem." "Remember the Lord afar off, and let Jerusalem come into your mind," was God's message to His dispersed people; "Look upon Zion." "The joy of Jerusalem was heard even afar off," the Spirit records of the rejoicings that followed the rebuilding of the walls of the city; and the joy of the Heavenly City may cheer our pilgrim hearts even now. (Col. 3:2; Ps. 25:15; Dan. 6:10; Jer. 51:50; Isa. 33:20; Neh. 12:43)

"Behold, I create Jerusalem a rejoicing, and her people a joy," God declared through His prophet Isaiah. "Thou shalt call thy walls Salvation, and thy gates Praise. The sun shall be no more thy light by day; neither for brightness shall the moon give light unto thee: but the Lord shall be unto thee an everlasting light, and thy God thy glory. Thy sun shall no more go down; neither shall thy moon withdraw itself: for the Lord shall be thine everlasting light, and the days of thy mourning shall be ended." (Isa. 65:18; 60:18-20)

These fragrant words were written to people who had never seen Jerusalem, nor probably ever would; yet God urged them to think upon the city where He had been pleased to set His name, and promised if they did so that they would share in her blessings even in their dispersal. And shall not we who know the certainty and the reality of the New Jerusalem, whose glories one day we shall share, let Jerusalem come into our minds and think upon Zion to strengthen us on our way?

"When my thoughts wax warm about whither I am going," declared Christian, when asked by what measures he sought to overcome the trials of his pilgrim way, "*that* will do it!"[9]

God means us to live by the grace of heaven now. Shall we

not seek the aid of Jerusalem to help us bring forth the particular fruit of the Spirit that God requires of us?

Sweet are the songs of the Heavenly City, sung by those who have loved her afar off and have learned to walk in the light of her radiance. From his twelfth-century monastery cell Bernard of Cluny sang:

> There grief is turned to pleasure,
>   Such pleasure as below
> No human voice can utter,
>   No human heart can know;
> And now we fight the battle,
>   But then shall wear the crown
> Of full and everlasting
>   And passionless renown.
>
> The morning shall awaken,
>   The shadows flee away,
> And each true-hearted servant
>   Shall shine as doth the day;
> And God, our King and Portion,
>   In fulness of His grace,
> We then shall see forever,
>   And worship face to face.
>
> Thou hast no shore, fair ocean,
>   Thou hast no time, bright day,
> Dear Fountain of Refreshment
>   To pilgrims far away!
> Upon the Rock of Ages
>   They build thy holy tower:
> Thine is the victor's laurel,
>   And thine the golden dower.[41]

Heaven was real to James Montgomery, and he sang:

> My Father's house on high!
>   Home of the soul, how near

> At times to faith's foreseeing eye
>   Thy golden gates appear!
> Ah, then my spirit faints
>   To reach the land I love,
> The bright inheritance of saints,
>   Jerusalem above![33]

Thomas à Kempis foresaw with joy the redemption of the body:

> O how glorious and resplendent,
>   Fragile body, thou shalt be,
> When endued with so much beauty,
>   Full of health, and strong, and free,
> Full of vigour, full of pleasure,
>   Thou shalt last eternally![49]

Often it has been to His suffering saints that God has most clearly revealed the vision of His heavenly glory. Far in the antiquity of time, when no belief in immortality seemed to form any part of creed or sacred writings, Job from the midst of his torments was enabled to give utterance to the sublime words whose comfort and clarity have never been surpassed: "I know that my redeemer liveth, and that he shall stand at the latter day upon the earth: and though after my skin worms destroy this body, yet in my flesh shall I see God: whom I shall see for myself ... and not another." And it was to the beloved John, grown old and weary in suffering in his island banishment, that God gave the mighty apocalyptic vision which tells us most of what we know about heaven. Shall not we, too, through the pain of our hedged-in circumstances, reach out in faith and "take heaven" to be our own? (*Job 19:25-27*)

ALL THE WAY

All the way my Saviour leads me;
    What have I to ask beside?
Can I doubt His tender mercy,
    Who through life has been my Guide?
Heavenly peace, divinest comfort,
    Here by faith in Him to dwell!
For I know, whate'er befall me,
    Jesus doeth all things well.

All the way my Saviour leads me,
    Cheers each winding path I tread,
Gives me grace for every trial,
    Feeds me with the living Bread.
Though my weary steps may falter,
    And my soul athirst may be,
Gushing from the Rock before me,
    Lo! a spring of joy I see!

All the way my Saviour leads me;
    Oh, the fullness of His love!
Perfect rest to me is promised
    In my Father's house above.
When my spirit, clothed immortal,
    Wings its flight to realms of day,
This my song through endless age:
    "Jesus led me all the way!"[43]

31

SATISFIED!

As for me, I will behold thy face in righteousness: I shall be satisfied, when I awake, with thy likeness. (Ps. 17:15)

In 1 Kings 11:14-22 we are given the brief and somewhat enigmatic story of Hadad the Edomite, an adversary of Solomon, who, while still a child, had fled for safety to Egypt with some of his father's house. There he found great favor with Pharaoh, was married into the king's family, and reared his son in the royal palace. But when he heard that David was dead, "Hadad said to Pharaoh, Let me depart, that I may go to mine own country. Then Pharaoh said unto him, But what hast thou lacked with me, that, behold, thou seekest to go to thine own country? And he answered, Nothing: howbeit let me go in any wise." His was the longing of the exiled heart for home. (1 Kings 11:21-22)

Likewise, the true Christian carries in his exiled heart a hunger that can only be satisfied by the fullness of God Himself and by his own country—his soul's true home. "The eye is not satisfied with seeing, nor the ear filled with hearing"; always there is the yearning for something "other"—that something for which we were made and without which we shall never know true satisfaction—God Himself. (*Eccles. 1:8*)

God has ever been the Satisfier of His people. The Old Testament abounds with records of how God not only met the needs of His children, but satisfied them abundantly. And He is the same today. His satisfactions are not only for the future, but for the present—for now; and it is with His own fullness, His very Self, that He satisfies His own.

"My people shall be satisfied with my goodness," He has told us, and He promises that He will satisfy the longing soul and fill the hungry soul with goodness. Indeed, "our best fare here is hunger,"[17] for He has covenanted to satisfy our deepest needs abundantly. (*Jer. 31:14; Pss. 107:9; 22:26; Isa. 58:11*)

But the ultimate satisfaction for the believer, and that for which the whole of creation waits and longs, is the joy of beholding God's face, of awakening in His likeness. The long years of suffering and schooling are done; the conformity to the image of His Son, which has been the supreme purpose of our life on earth and the sole reason for the hedges with which He has encircled us, is complete; and fully and forever, and far beyond our highest imaginings, we shall be satisfied. "I shall be satisfied, when I awake, with thy likeness." (*Ps. 17:15*)

In that day we shall be satisfied with perfect understanding. "Now we see through a glass, darkly; but then face to face: now I know in part; but then shall I know even as also I am known." At last the meaning of our hedges will be made plain to us. Not that the sovereign God need explain Himself and His ways to His creatures even then; but we believe that in His grace He will. We shall understand His eternal plan and purpose and our own part in it, and we shall learn the particular form of service for which our hedges have prepared us. (*1 Cor. 13:12*)

Will not the End explain
The crossed endeavour, earnest purpose foiled,
The strange bewilderment of good work spoiled,
The clinging weariness, the inward strain,
Will not the End explain?

Meanwhile He comforteth
Them that are losing patience; 'tis His way.
But none can write the words they hear Him say
For men to read; only they know He saith
Kind words, and comforteth.

Not that He doth explain
The mystery that baffleth; but a sense
Husheth the quiet heart, that far, far hence
Lieth a field set thick with golden grain
Wetted in seedling days by many a rain;
The End, it will explain.[3]

The comforts that He gives us now, wordless and wonderful, will be ours in perfect satisfaction and understanding in that day.

Not only shall we understand our hedges, but we shall at last understand ourselves and one another. The mysteries of personality will be made plain, and we shall unfold endlessly the delights of perfected individuality and fellowship. There we shall be forever united with those we have known and loved on earth; there we shall enter into the joys of fellowship with the redeemed of all ages. With joy and freedom we shall share in the blessed community of service and praise, satisfied at last with perfect understanding!

In that day we shall be satisfied with perfect knowledge. Earth's vast unsounded treasury of learning, whose pursuit affords such keen delights to the human mind, will be but as a shallow pool compared to the shoreless sea of wonders we shall explore in heaven. All the glories of music, language, and art, the wonders of science and invention, the unfathomable mysteries of the universe, the riddles of God's dealings with man in history, the mathematics of the universe, the literature of the eternal ages—all the lovely and elusive endeavors we have loved and followed here will then be known to perfection. We shall not have to search within ourselves for creativity nor seek for newness of expression; creativity will flow from us as rivers of water, for what is God but eternal and perfect creativity? And we shall be satisfied by sharing in the very life of God.

In that day we shall be satisfied with perfect service. "His servants shall serve Him" at last. We who on earth have so imperfectly served Him, we who because of our hedges have had to forego so much activity and service of any kind, shall be satisfied in that day by serving Him fully and freely, endlessly and effortlessly. What will His service be? Who can tell? Purest worship, perfect praise, and creative activity of infinite variety and unimaginable joy and glory. All that we know on earth of beauty is but a dim reflection of the One who within Himself encompasses the perfection of all Beauty; and beauty will then be ours not only to enjoy, but to create. What will it be to be freed to serve Him at last, and in magnificent capacity bounded only by the limits of His own limitless nature! (Rev. 22:3)

Such service will be possible in that day because we shall at last be satisfied with perfect holiness. "We shall be like him; for we shall see him as he is." Perfect sinlessness will be ours—forever. Gone will be the failures and defeats that mark our spiritual pilgrimage here. Perfected, complete, we shall stand before Him: perfectly conformed to His image, perfectly to love Him, perfectly to praise Him, perfectly to do His holy will. Fully and forever, we shall be complete in Him. This is the destiny in store for the children of God; and with His likeness we shall, indeed, be satisfied. (1 John 3:2)

And "there shall be no more curse." The aged John, viewing the glories of heaven from the confines of the lonely island where he had spent so many years of imprisonment, wrote of the dissolution of his particular hedge in the words "and there was no more sea." Each of us may write in place of "sea" the name of our own specific hedge and know that the word is true, for there will be no more hedges. Whatever it is that has closed us away from the fullness of life on earth—pain, weakness, mental illness, sorrow, disappointment, heartbreak, tragedy, or trouble of whatever kind—all shall be done away with forever, and life in unspeakable fullness will be ours, life everlasting and abundant, even the very life of God Himself. And with His fullness we shall be satisfied. (Rev. 22:3; 21:1)

Will He, too, be satisfied in that day? Will the Savior see the travail of His soul in us and be fully satisfied? Or must both He and we enter upon the endless ages of eternity knowing something less than the perfect satisfaction He has planned because we have not allowed Him to complete in us, through His hedge of suffering, that conformity to His likeness for which He had designed it? (Isa. 53:11)

"To him that overcometh will I give . . . a white stone, and in the stone a new name written, which no man knoweth saving he that receiveth it." May not that new name, forever secret between our souls and God, be the measure of His satisfaction in us? Oh, to be prepared to be fit partakers of the glory that will be revealed, even though it be by sharing in Christ's sufferings now! For the morning is coming, and with it the satisfaction of His presence and His fullness. (Rev. 2:17)

'Midst the darkness, storm and sorrow,
    One bright gleam I see:
Well I know the blessed morrow
    Christ will come for me.
'Midst the light and peace and glory
    Of His Father's home,
Christ for me is watching, waiting,
    Waiting till I come.

Long the blessed Guide has led me
   By the desert road;
Now I see the golden towers,
   City of my God.
There amidst the love and glory
   He is waiting yet;
On His hands a name is graven
   He can ne'er forget.

There, amidst the songs of heaven,
   Sweeter to His ear
Is the footfall through the desert,
   Ever drawing near.
There, made ready, are the mansions,
   Radiant, still, and fair;
But the Bride the Father gave Him
   Yet is wanting there.

Who is this who comes to meet me
   On the desert way,
As the Morning Star, foretelling
   God's unclouded day?
He it is who came to win me
   On the cross of shame;
In His glory well I know Him,
   Evermore the same.

Oh, the blessed joy of meeting,
   All the desert past;
Oh, the wondrous words of greeting
   He shall speak at last!
He and I together entering
   Those fair courts above;
He and I together sharing
   All the Father's love!

Where no shade nor stain can enter,
   Nor the gold be dim,
In that holiness unsullied,
   I shall walk with Him.

Meet companion then for Jesus,
　　From Him, for Him, made;
Glory of God's grace forever
　　There in me displayed!

He who in His hour of sorrow
　　Bore the curse alone;
I who through the lonely desert
　　Trod where He had gone;
He and I, in that bright glory,
　　One deep joy shall share—
Mine, to be forever with Him;
　　His, that I am there.[44]

SOURCES AND ACKNOWLEDGMENTS

[1]E. Margaret Clarkson.
[2]Frederick W. H. Myers (1843-1901), from *St. Paul.*
[3]Amy Carmichael (1867-1951).
[4]Juliana of Norwich (1342-c.1413), from *Revelations of Divine Love.*
[5]Samuel Rodigast (1649-1708), tr. by Catherine Winkworth (1829-1878).
[6]Gerhardt Tersteegen (1697-1763), from *The Quiet Way,* letters of Tersteegen, tr. by Emily Chisholm. Used by permission of Philosophical Library, Inc.
[7]William Hiley Bathurst (1796-1877).
[8]Author and source unknown.
[9]John Bunyan (1628-1688), from *Pilgrim's Progress.*
[10]St. Patrick (374-466), tr. by Cecil Frances Alexander (1818-1895).
[11]Anna L. Waring (1820-1910).
[12]Alexander Whyte (1836-1921), from *Samuel Rutherford and Some of His Correspondents.*
[13]Alexander Cruden (1701-1770), from *Cruden's Concordance.*
[14]Frederick William Faber (1814-1863).
[15]Elizabeth Barrett Browning (1806-1861), from "Cowper's Grave."
[16]"God's Purpose in Pain," from *HIS* magazine. Used by permission.
[17]Samuel Rutherford (1600-1661), from *Letters.*
[18]Christina Rossetti (1830-1894).
[19]The Nicene Creed.
[20]John Milton (1608-1674), from *Paradise Lost,* Book 1.
[21]Dr. William Fitch, from *God and Evil.* Used by permission from Wm. B. Eerdmans Publishing Co.
[22]Michael Bruce (1746-1767).
[23]E.E.H., Keswick Hymn Book.
[24]Harriet Eleanor Hamilton King (1840-1920), "Ugo Bassi's Sermon in the Hospital," from *The Disciples.*

[25]Dr. William Culbertson, from *Moody Monthly*. Used by permission.
[26]Augustus Montague Toplady (1740-1778).
[27]Henry Francis Lyte (1793-1847).
[28]The Shorter Catechism.
[29]Rev. Albert Seigle.
[30]*The Cloud of Unknowing*, Penguin Classics.
[31]Anne Ross Cousin (1824-1906).
[32]Title of sermon preached by Rev. David Howard, Knox Church, Toronto.
[33]James Montgomery (1771-1854).
[34]C. S. Lewis (1898-1963), from *The Screwtape Letters*, Chapter 8; *Letters to Malcolm*, Chapter 21.
[35]Title of a sermon preached by Dr. William Fitch, Knox Church, Toronto, Thanksgiving, 1965.
[36]Horatius Bonar (1808-1889).
[37]Frances Ridley Havergal (1836-1879).
[38]Paraphrased from Alan M. Stibbs, *The New Bible Commentary*.
[39]Isaac Watts (1674-1748).
[40]Karl Johann Philipp Spitta (1801-1859), tr. by C. T. Ashley (1825—).
[41]Bernard of Cluny (12th century), tr. by John Mason Neale (1818-1866).
[42]William Walsham Howe (1823-1897).
[43]Fanny J. Crosby (1823-1915).
[44]Gerhardt Tersteegen (1697-1763), from "The Bride."
[45]Charles Wesley (1707-1788).
[46]19th Century German, tr. by Edward Caswall (1814-1878).
[47]John Newton (1725-1807).
[48]Annie Johnson Flint (1866-1932).
[49]Thomas à Kempis (c.1380-1471), tr. by John Mason Neale (1818-1865).